Screen Works

Screen Works

**PRACTICAL AND
INSPIRATIONAL
IDEAS FOR
MAKING
AND USING
SCREENS IN THE
HOME**

MARION ELLIOT

SPECIAL PHOTOGRAPHY
BY TIM IMRIE

HERMES
HOUSE

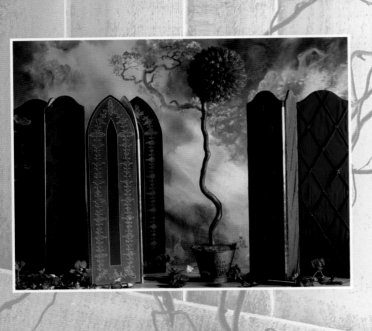

This edition published by Hermes House
an imprint of
Anness Publishing Limited
Hermes House
88-89 Blackfriars Road
London SE1 8HA

A CIP catalogue record for this book is available from the British Library

ISBN 1 84038 444 1

Publisher: Joanna Lorenz
Project Editor: Judith Simons
Photographer: Tim Imrie
Step Photographer: John Freeman
Stylist: Fannie Ward
Designer: Lisa Tai
Illustrator: Lucinda Ganderton

Printed and bound in Singapore

© Anness Publishing Limited 1997
Updated © 1999

3 5 7 9 10 8 6 4

Contents

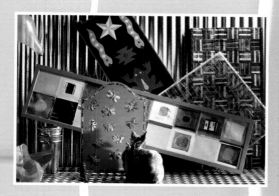

Introduction

A SCREEN IS ONE OF THE SIMPLEST DEVICES FOR TRANSFORMING A ROOM. SCREENS HAVE MASSIVE POTENTIAL FOR RESHAPING, REDEFINING AND REDESIGNING YOUR LIVING SPACE, CREATING DRAMATIC CONTRASTS OR QUIET CORNERS, DIFFUSING DAYLIGHT, HIDING UGLY CLUTTER AND DIVIDING INTERIORS TO MAXIMIZE SPACE.

A SCREEN CAN ALSO BE A DRAMATIC DESIGN VEHICLE, ADDING A SPLASH OF OPULENCE, PARED-DOWN MINIMALISM, ORIENTAL GRANDEUR OR COUNTRY SIMPLICITY TO A ROOM, AND THUS ALLOWING INSTANT CHANGES OF ATMOSPHERE ACCORDING TO YOUR MOOD. ALMOST ANY DESIGN, STYLE OR COLOUR COMBINATION CAN BE USED TO EMBELLISH A SCREEN — THINK OF IT AS A BLANK CANVAS TO DECORATE FOR INSTANT IMPACT, AND THEN REVISE THE CHOICE OF DECORATION AS YOUR INTERIOR STYLE EVOLVES.

History of **screens**

The history of screens is a long and varied one. Like many innovations, they are thought to have originated in China, and they have been in general use in the East for more than 2000 years. Chinese screens were imposing structures formed from many heavily lacquered wooden panels. These were often inlaid with precious materials such as jade and silver, and lavishly decorated with incised and painted designs.

The idea of the screen was wholeheartedly embraced by the Japanese when it was introduced from China, and it was immediately adapted to complement the traditional Japanese way of life. One of the most significant Japanese additions was the use of handmade paper to cover a lightweight wooden framework, which made their screens much more portable than the Chinese versions. Each panel of a Chinese screen was usually illustrated with a separate decorative scene, but the Japanese tended to treat the combined surface of the panels as one large canvas that they covered with bold compositions depicting natural and domestic scenes. This allowed a touch of decoration to be introduced into the rather austere Japanese interior.

Japanese screens were originally designed as dividers to partition the grand halls of important houses into smaller areas. They were also used in more modest dwellings, and specific styles of screen were developed for different functions.

Right: A Chinese black lacquer screen is embellished with silver and gilt decoration. Screens are thought to have originated in China, and early examples were particularly imposing with as many as 20 folding panels.

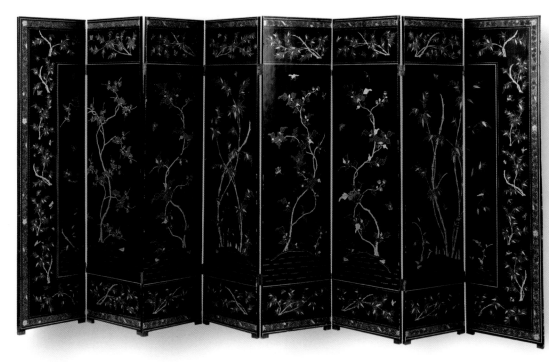

Below: The Japanese adapted the Chinese prototype to suit their own requirements and décor. Their folding screens were constructed from panels covered with sheets of handmade paper, making them easy to move from one location to another.

Traditional Japanese houses are uncluttered and very open, so screens were useful for blocking draughts and creating intimacy. The "Fusuma", a large wood-and-paper structure that ran in grooves in the floor, was designed to slide open and shut. It was, in effect, a moveable wall that could be used either to create one large, open room or to divide the space into separate areas. The paper panels attached to the trellis-like wooden structure diffused natural light to create a soft, hazy effect. Another common screen was the "Byobu" (literally "protection from the wind"), a folding screen with up to six panels and wooden frames covered with sturdy paper. The panels were hinged together by the paper, and were light enough to be carried quite easily. This made "Byobu" screens very versatile, and they were used in the home and also during important ceremonies.

The most common screens – lacquered and highly decorative, with naturalistic subject matter picked out in gold on a dark background – were not known in Europe until the 17th century, when trade routes were established between the Orient and the West. However, other screens were used in Europe before this time. Kitchens in great houses were screened from the banqueting hall by wooden structures, and free-standing screens supported on wooden stands were used as protection from draughts and the heat of open fires.

Folding screens did exist at this time, but probably more significant were the curtains and drapes used to screen beds, from medieval times onwards. These were often considerably more luxurious than the beds themselves, and were an absolute necessity to protect the occupants from the bitter cold of large, unheated rooms. Richly embroidered panels were often displayed behind the bed, and flowing cloth canopies cascaded around the bed frame to create a private space. By the 15th century, curtains had become an integral part of the bed rather than being suspended from walls and ceilings.

During the 17th century the screen, whether folding or rigid, came into its own as an important item of furniture in Europe. All kinds of materials were used, including rich velvets, tapestry, leather and, eventually, as trade routes were established with the Orient, lacquer. One result of the influx of Western traders and missionaries into Japan was the Namban style of art, in which Japanese artists mixed elements of Eastern and Western culture to produce European subject matter in a Japanese style. A wide range of items, principally screens, was decorated in this way: common motifs included European merchants and their ships.

Screens, along with china, fabrics and printed papers, were exported from East to West, starting a flourishing market for Eastern wares, which were now seen by Western eyes for the first time. The impact of this trade was tremendous, and Eastern goods were much imitated by European craftsmen who were now fighting to hold on to their position in manufacturing. The craze for chinoiserie, a hybrid of Eastern motifs and Western style, led to a flourishing European industry that manufactured a wide range of goods, including folding screens. The Europeans devised their own method of lacquering, known as "japanning", which was a cheaper, quicker alternative to the oriental process. Oriental craftsmen were also encouraged to produce subject matter with a European slant to make their wares more acceptable to Western tastes.

Screens became very fashionable throughout Europe, with different countries stamping their own style on the basic form. Britain, and more especially France, became centres of

Above left: This ornate gilded screen with unusual glass panels was made to grace an aristocratic interior. From the 17th century, screens became very fashionable *throughout Europe and were crafted to reflect the prevailing style in other items of furniture.*

Above right: Made for an Irish magistrate, this magnificent screen dates from the 18th century. The British were particularly fond of screens that *depicted naturalistic scenes, and sporting screens like this one epitomize the style.*

Left: *This deep red lacquer screen was made by Eileen Gray c. 1923. Gray, an influential designer, studied and perfected the art of lacquering with a Japanese craftsman.*

appeared, with an adjustable panel that slid up and down a wooden pole to provide screening at the right height.

The folding screen seems to have fallen from favour as an item of furniture in European homes by the beginning of the 19th century, but a resurgence of interest in Japanese art and design in the latter half of the century brought it to the attention of artists and craftsmen once more, and hugely influential designers such as William Morris explored the form. Morris produced a number of screens, including folding ones with tapestry panels in the medieval style.

As screens began to be appreciated as art objects rather than simply as utilitarian items of furniture, many more painters and designers decorated them. In the 20th century artists such as Bernard Buffet, and Vanessa Bell and Duncan Grant at the Omega Workshops, were inspired to work on screens, and the designer Eileen Gray studied the art of lacquering with a Japanese master-craftsman.

excellence for lacquerware, with the French producing work to rival that of the Japanese. The Dutch raised the art of stamping and gilding leather to an art form, creating leather-panelled screens of great sophistication and beauty. In Italy and France, craftsmen produced screens with rococo-inspired carved frames of great opulence to grace royal palaces such as Versailles. As the screen became a well-established item of furniture, its form and decoration followed whatever style was currently in vogue, with panel shapes, colour, materials and size changing according to the prevailing fashion.

Not all screens had multiple panels – very popular from the 18th century on were single-panel firescreens. Although such screens had been used since medieval times, they now became more sophisticated in both design and function. It was common practice to huddle around open fires, but the basket grates used in fireplaces at this time produced such a fierce heat that it was necessary to protect people from scorching themselves. The cheval, or horse, firescreen was a solid, flat, single panel supported on two crossways feet. It could be moved around to provide the most effective screening of direct heat while still allowing warm air to circulate freely. In some cheval screens, the central panel slid up and down. Slightly later the pole screen

Above: *A screen depicting Parisian landmarks, including Le Sacré Coeur, Eiffel Tower, Moulin Rouge and Sainte Chapelle, by Bernard Buffet.*

Types of **screen**

From the lightweight, paper-covered frameworks of Japan to the gilded rococo examples of the French boudoir, most cultures have their own version of the screen. A screen can take many forms, be it a simple fabric room divider or a multi-panel folding screen, but the function is the same: to hide, or to shield from extremes of temperature.

The first screens, the mighty lacquered Chinese screens, had enormous panels of up to 3 m (10 ft). The number of panels was always even, sometimes totalling more than 20. They were used to divide great halls in important houses and palaces, hence their great size. This type of screen was exported to the West when trade routes opened in the 17th century, and was used in the mansions of Europe. However, the insatiable desire for chinoiserie led to smaller panels being produced for export, and lacquered boards were even made specifically to be cut up and incorporated into panelled furniture and walls.

The advent of these oriental screens established the folding screen as a staple of the fashionable household. Prior to this, folding screens did exist in Europe, but they were less common

and were frequently covered with rich fabrics such as velvet and silk, rather than being painted.

Japanese screens were also exported to Europe in the 17th century. Folding screens ("Byobu") usually had no more than six panels; the framework was lightweight wood, and strong handmade paper was used to cover the panels. The Japanese also developed the "Fusuma", a sliding wall panel that could be opened and closed to divide or close off sections of their large open-plan rooms.

Ornate metal and wooden screens have long existed in the Middle East, in India and in North African countries such as Morocco. These screens are mostly single panels, and were placed at open windows or on verandahs to provide some privacy. The idea of confusing the eye with intricate pattern is also practised in the architecture of these countries, and pierced stonework in a dazzling array of geometric designs is used to conceal enclosed gardens and terraces.

Another Middle Eastern innovation was the stamped, painted and gilded leather hanging, a device that had decorated

Left: *This is a typical mahogany and needlepoint pole screen with tripod feet. The single panel is adjustable, allowing it to be moved up and down the pole either to screen the heat of an open fire or to block a draught.*

Right: *An ornately carved cheval firescreen like this was once a common sight in grand houses. With some screens, the central panel could be adjusted. The cheval screen was eventually superseded by the pole screen.*

Left: *Lengths of heavy fabric and ornate tapestries were suspended around grand beds to protect the occupants from the pervasive cold associated with castles and large houses. Curtains eventually became an integral part of beds, creating small enclosed "rooms".*

European walls from medieval times and was eventually incorporated into folding screens. From Moorish Spain, the technique of leather gilding spread through Europe, with the Dutch and Flemish in particular adopting the technique and producing finely decorated screens.

The English, French and Italians were all enthusiastic exponents of the folding screen. All three countries practised the art of lacquering in the oriental style, and France became an important centre for the technique. As well as oriental influences, each country produced its own unique screens, with stylistic innovations peculiar to its culture. While they all produced painted screens, the British favoured naturalistic depictions of rural scenes and pastimes, often in moderately decorative frames. The French and Italians, on the other hand, favoured a more theatrical approach, covering their screens with finely painted panels encased in heavily carved and gilded frames in the rococo style. Lengths of tapestry, silk, printed

paper and half-panels of glass, mirror and pierced wood were also incorporated into European screens with great enthusiasm.

Apart from folding screens, there were also firescreens, in the form of single panels. The earliest style was the cheval, or horse, screen. This was short and sturdy, and often ornately carved, with a tapestry panel that could be raised and lowered. A more sophisticated firescreen, the pole screen, superseded the cheval screen during the early 18th century. This type of screen was supported on long, slender poles with tripod feet, and had an adjustable panel that could be moved up and down to protect people from the intense heat of an open fire.

A variation on the firescreen was the fire, or chimney, board. This was fitted into the recess of an empty fireplace during the summer months to screen the space, providing a decorative focal point and blocking draughts. The boards were painted with designs of varying degrees of sophistication – often vases of flowers or bowls of fruit – to give a *trompe-l'oeil* effect.

Materials used

The prototype for all screens, the folding Chinese screen, was a large structure made from wood that was heavily lacquered and decorated in a variety of ways. The heavy wooden panels had a self-contained design and were hinged together with leather or fabric strips.

Chinese lacquer was obtained from tree resin. It was a thick, grey substance that darkened on contact with the air, and it could be stained with pigments to produce a wide range of bright colours. The wooden screen panels were very carefully prepared before the lacquer was applied. Each panel was coated with paper or fabric to create a ground. Then, as many as 20 or 30 coats of lacquer were brushed on, with several days allowed for drying between each coat. When the desired depth of colour was achieved, the panels were painstakingly polished to a subtle, shiny finish.

The most widely exported Chinese screen, the "Coromandel" (so-called because Coromandel on the coast of southern India was an important stopping-off point on the East–West trade

Above: This is a typical Dutch folding screen with embossed leather panels. Moorish leather wall hangings were much admired in Europe and this method of decorating leather was adapted by the Dutch and Flemish to produce ornate room dividers and screens.

Left: An eight-panel Chinese "Coromandel" shows the incised decoration associated with this type of screen. The design was cut directly into each lacquered panel, then inlaid with coloured lacquer and precious materials.

route), was decorated with an incised pattern that was cut directly into the lacquered panels. The recessed designs were then filled in with bright colours and gilt or gold dust. Other materials used to decorate Chinese screens included silver, mother-of-pearl, jade and shell.

Japanese screens, though based on their Chinese predecessors, were more ingeniously constructed. A lightweight wooden framework of up to six panels was covered with handmade paper and paper fibres to make a translucent screen. The paper was skilfully interwoven from panel to panel to make sealed hinges that opened in both directions. This provided a continuous expanse of paper that could be decorated across its whole surface with one design, rather than in self-contained panels like the Chinese screens. The Japanese also decorated their screens with low-relief designs made with a thick paste. Both Chinese and Japanese screens were decorated with subject matter that included scenes of everyday life, plants, animals and landscapes. Japanese screens were generally smaller and lighter than the Chinese ones and could therefore be moved quite easily.

European screens made in the oriental style were "japanned": that is, decorated with an approximation of Chinese lacquer. It was impossible to export the lacquer from China, as it started to darken as soon as it was exposed to the air, but a cheaper alternative was produced by Italian and Dutch craftsmen, and was widely used.

Many other materials and techniques were employed to produce and decorate screens. From medieval times, wood and wicker screens were used to divide rooms, as were sumptuous tapestry hangings that were suspended around beds to keep out draughts. Similar hangings and panels were made from gilded and painted or punched leather, which were also used as screen panels. The greatest exponents of leather screens were the Dutch and Flemish, who produced screens with oriental-inspired motifs as well as more traditional designs.

By the mid-18th century, painted leather and canvas screens – often decorated with pastoral scenes – were produced in great numbers. They could also be covered with panels of printed "India" paper that was decorated with repeating patterns of chinoiserie flowers and figures.

At this time, almost any kind of material was used to cover screens or to be set into panels. Frames were made from a variety of woods, including walnut and mahogany. They were often intricately carved, especially in Italy and France, where Louis

Above: *This beautiful pole screen is now used as a decorative ornament rather than for any practical purpose. Pole screens were framed with intricately carved wood, containing a patterned silk or needlepoint panel.*

XV's love of rococo resulted in the production of dazzlingly ornate surrounds that were frequently gilded. Louis XVI went one step further by ordering a screen whose frame was actually cast from gilt bronze rather than being gilded. Painted silks, tapestries, marquetry and sumptuous fabrics were all employed in the decoration of French screens, turning them into some of the most elegant and beautiful ever made.

Design elements

Whatever the proportions and layout of your home, any room can be transformed with a screen. Nowadays the word "screen" need not denote a lacquered and gilded rococo fantasy; it merely refers to a device for blocking off or dividing a space. A contemporary screen could be as simple as a length of muslin draped over a wooden curtain pole.

Before choosing the style of your screen, decide what function it is to fulfil. Will it be used for hiding an untidy area? Or do you wish to create a room within a room, to make a haven of privacy in a quiet corner? Perhaps space is a problem, and you would like to divide a studio flat to create the illusion of two rooms where there is only one. Any of these issues can be addressed with the right type of screen. More than one solution may be appropriate, depending on the amount of space you have, the existing décor, and whether the screen is to be a permanent fixture or a moveable object.

Above: *Often a rather dull, if necessary, screening device, the shower curtain can become a watery wonder with the addition of a few shells and bundles of driftwood.*

In modern homes it is not of overriding importance to block draughts, one of the original functions of traditional folding screens. However, this type of screen always adds an air of sophistication to a room and, being portable, is immensely practical. This allows for the regular rearrangement of the room to create new and different perspectives and, of course, the screen can simply be taken with you if you move.

Solid-panel folding screens can be decorated with paint, paper, found objects and fabric to create any effect you like. For example, a sprinkling of gold stars applied with a rubber stamp can give a richly coloured screen Byzantine splendour, while a distressed paint effect in shades of cool blue-green will create a Scandinavian look – a stylish complement to stripped wood and natural floor coverings. Solid panels can also be covered with fabric, ranging from hessian or cotton ticking to watered satin, tapestry and brocade, to create a huge range of formal and informal effects, suitable for every room. Open-panel screens can be used to convey a variety of looks – a lick of paint and a length of fabric or paper are all that is needed to achieve anything from Gothic splendour to minimalist simplicity.

Above: *Lengths of vivid sari fabric have been used to create a filmy screen around a four-poster bed. The effect is purely decorative, with little need these days for the draught-defeating capabilities of early bed screens.*

As well as traditional moveable screens, there are static room dividers that remain *in situ* but can be opened and closed, tied back and rolled up to ring the changes. These include that simplest of screens, the humble plastic shower curtain, jazzed up with a row of artificial shells and lengths of driftwood suspended along its width using raffia. Then there are wide, tab-topped curtains in every colour imaginable that can be suspended across the width of a room to create two distinct areas, lengths of muslin clipped to tension wire to divide a large space, and sari fabrics hung around a bed to provide a tranquil sleeping area.

Above: *For a touch of rustic charm, screen a tin bath by arranging bath towels over a wooden drier. Adapt the idea for a modern bathroom, using pretty linens and lace panels on decorative freestanding driers.*

Some screens are entirely spontaneous, created out of necessity on the spur of the moment; for example, a heavy woollen blanket pinned around a bed on a chilly night, towels hung around a bath tub on a towel airer to preserve a bather's modesty, or a room simply divided with a sheet when an unexpected guest comes to stay.

Screens in the Home

THERE ARE SO MANY WAYS TO
USE SCREENS IN THE HOME —
TO ENHANCE, TO DIVIDE OR
TO EVOKE ATMOSPHERE — THAT IT IS
SOMETIMES DIFFICULT TO KNOW WHERE
TO BEGIN. FROM PRE-CUT BLANKS TO
DUSTSHEET DIVIDERS, THE CHOICE OF
BASIC MATERIALS SEEMS ENORMOUS.
HOWEVER, ONCE YOU HAVE DECIDED ON
THE LOOK THAT IS BEST SUITED TO
YOUR LIVING SPACE, OTHER
CONSIDERATIONS SUCH AS COLOUR,
PATTERN, TEXTURE, SIZE AND SHAPE
WILL FALL INTO PLACE, ALLOWING YOUR
SCREEN TO BE AS STYLISH AND
INNOVATIVE AS YOU PLEASE.

Screens as dividers

An interior living space is seldom perfect. It may be the size of a pocket handkerchief, yet have good light. It may have to accommodate several activities on the same level at the same time, or may be an annoying collection of odd angles and wasted corners. Yet, with a little thought, a multitude of sins can be righted or at least diminished by using some kind of room divider.

The most dramatic, and simplest, type of room divider can be created by suspending a length of utilitarian fabric from a pole or a line of tension wire. Some of the cheapest fabrics are also the most elegant. A wide length of loosely woven, scratchy hessian with its distinctive, slightly oily aroma has a timeless chic that will complement almost any interior. The same goes for cotton mattress ticking and heavy-duty unbleached calico. All these fabrics are much wider than average and will not even need sewing. For a more styled look, search out interesting curtain clips in wrought iron and chrome, or embellish the fabric with curtain weights sewn on the right side of the divider, or with mother-of-pearl or wooden buttons. Some fabrics, such as heavy calico, may need more support than a line of wire. There is a wide range of curtain poles and finials available in wood and iron; alternatively you can make your own from a broom handle and buy the fixings from a hardware store.

If you plan to create the illusion of two rooms where there is only one, or to hide a work area from view, it is obviously important to do so without blocking all the

Above: *This type of screen will not protect from draughts, but makes a strong visual divider, clearly defining different areas of the room. The paper is translucent, allowing light to diffuse beautifully.*

natural light from one or other area. This is where paper comes into its own as a room divider – chosen and suspended with care, it will provide the requisite screening effect while still allowing in light.

Thin, lightweight papers make the best light-diffusing room dividers. There are many available, from rolls of greaseproof or tracing paper to handmade papers embedded with flower heads. Thin paper need not be flimsy – some Japanese papers made from plant fibres such as mulberry and gampi are very sheer yet incredibly strong, owing to the length of the fibres used. They also look very attractive suspended in the light, revealing the snaking pattern made by the fibres.

Above: *Simple materials can be used to stunning effect. Here, a wooden garden trellis and sheets of tracing paper combine to make a hanging screen that is both functional and very stylish.*

To make a paper room divider, simply drape strips or whole sheets of paper over wire, cardboard tubes, string or a curtain pole. If the paper is very light, glue washers or curtain weights to the lower edges. The beauty of this kind of room divider is that you can change the paper whenever it starts to look tatty or you tire of it, and for very little cost.

Another stylish room divider can be made by attaching squares of heavy tracing paper to the back of a wooden garden

Above: *Create an instant divider by suspending a length of unbleached calico from a curtain pole or tension wire. This look works particularly well in a simple, elegant space such as a loft room.*

trellis, in imitation of traditional Japanese wall screens. The paper is just opaque enough to provide some privacy, while still letting light into the room. This kind of screen looks stunning in an airy space against a pale wall.

Functional **screens**

Central heating and modern insulation have virtually robbed screens of their role as protectors from draughts and fires, but contemporary screens should not just be seen as decorative white elephants. There are many types of screens, room dividers and light diffusers, and some are supremely functional as well as very attractive.

The perennial problem of how to disguise the gaping hole of an empty fireplace during the summer months was neatly solved during the 17th century by the advent of the chimney board. This was a wooden panel – bearing a decorative motif such as a

bowl of fruit or flowers – that fitted into the recess of the fireplace, blocking draughts and providing a pleasant focal point. This idea can be imitated by propping an attractively framed painting in an empty grate for the duration of the summer until it is time to set the fire once more. Depending on its size, a painting may also prevent heat from escaping through the fireplace and draughts from coming in.

Safety is always an important consideration with open fires, especially with small children; it is usually essential to place a guard, and preferably one that fixes to the wall or fireplace surround, in front of the fire to prevent accidents. Metal mesh guards are perfectly adequate, but they are often not very stylish. There are, however, modern metal versions of the cheval screen,

Above: *An open fireplace can look very bare during the summer months. Reinstate it as a focal point within the room by propping a favourite painting in front of the grate.*

Left: *A window recess can be transformed into a tranquil reading corner by simply enclosing it with filmy curtains. These beautiful drapes have been made from Indian saris.*

the single-panelled screen that was placed before a fire in the 17th century. Frequently Indian or North African in origin, designs include a pierced metal panel intricately cut into a riot of flower and animal motifs, or a mesh of wrought iron worked into sturdy curlicues. Screens of this type can simply be placed in front of the fireplace, hiding the necessary mesh fireguard while allowing the heat to escape.

Screens are not just for hiding things. They can also be used to create an enclosed space – a little oasis of privacy and a retreat from the outside world. Sheer fabrics such as sari lengths in hot, spicy tones can be loosely draped to enclose a window recess, making a filmy corner for reading. Use more than one layer of fabric, building up a deep intensity of colour. Sew simple tabs

along the tops of the saris – metal curtain clips will do the job just as well – so that you can suspend the drapes from a metal pole. If you are really in a hurry, simply knot the fabric around a curtain pole or clip it from a line or wire with clothes pegs.

A practical and very decorative idea for the summer is to drape lengths of sheer muslin around a mosquito-net frame or plastic hula hoop and suspend it above the bed. This will keep away flies and mosquitoes, and will create a calm, cool atmosphere that is very relaxing.

Below: *A sturdy wrought-iron firescreen serves two purposes. It makes a pleasing alternative to utilitarian mesh fireguards, yet still allows the heat to escape.*

Quick-and-easy **screens**

The humblest and quirkiest of materials can be used to make screens that are both stylish and functional. In fact, some of the simplest materials work best if they are incorporated in an unusual or witty way that, nevertheless, looks entirely natural.

If you need to make a screen in a hurry, it is usually to divide a room for impromptu sleeping arrangements or to provide privacy. This is often the case in a new home before the curtains are ready, especially if the room is overlooked by other houses. The following simple ideas will quickly solve such problems and, as an added bonus, they are inexpensive too.

Virtually all types of paper are good for screening windows. Handmade papers, with their interesting and irregular appearance, make excellent screens as these qualities are intensified when strong daylight passes through them. Some Japanese papers, for instance, are made with long plant fibres that can be seen swirling under the surface. Coconut fibres make loosely bonded "paper" that is dense enough to block the view, yet open enough to let in chinks of light. Extra materials such as leaves, flower heads, onion skins, glitter and shredded newspaper can be added to other papers and look wonderful against the light.

Flowers always make a difference to a room, instantly bringing life to any interior. Instead of a dull net curtain, stuff silk flowers (or real ones for a temporary effect) into tall vases and line them up on a windowsill to make a bright display that will screen an ugly view. A wire rack containing rows of pot plants placed before

Above: *Handmade paper, embedded with flowers, can be hung in a window recess using metal clips from stationers. The paper diffuses the light and adds a delicate floral touch.*

Above: *Cheap, utilitarian materials can look extremely effective. Here a roll of corrugated cardboard, suspended from a length of wooden dowel and tied with tapes, makes an impromptu roller blind.*

Opposite: *Screens can be fun! Here, rows of plastic fruits and vegetables have been casually strung across a stable-type door to block out direct sunlight – a visual joke for the kitchen.*

the window would have the same effect, as would a collection of tall cacti or exotic dried flowers.

A fun idea is to suspend strings of plastic fruit along the lower half of a kitchen sash window. Bright and cheerful, they are also ideal for screening off a gap below a work surface or an alcove used for storage. Catering specialists also sell plastic crabs, shells, fish and lobsters intended for fishmongers' displays. These can be used to great effect in a bathroom – try stringing them together to make a crazy shower curtain!

Beach mats, available every summer at seaside stalls, make very stylish contemporary screens around a four-poster bed. Simply fold them over the top struts of the bed and hold them in place

Right: *Universally available and extremely cheap, plastic strip curtains provide shade and privacy, and keep flies at bay. They can also look distinctly stylish in the right setting and with the right accessories.*
Below left: *Strings of plastic beads enhance a doorway, providing privacy while allowing air to circulate.*
Below right: *A sheer fabric with lace edging makes an attractive temporary screen for a cottage window.*

for instant privacy, or pin it over a doorway or window to keep away flies, for example when cooking. The holes in the lace can be used if a more permanent screen is desired: simply suspend the tablecloth or shawl across a window on curtain wire threaded through the lace edging, to make a kind of café curtain. You can also suspend crocheted blankets over windows or around beds to keep out cold draughts during the winter.

Brightly coloured plastic strip curtains, seen in many a café doorway, are useful for both doors and windows. They are designed to keep out flies and other pests (indeed, some are impregnated with insecticide), and they allow air to circulate through a room while also providing a little shade. Plastic strip curtains are very cheap and widely available, and they can be grouped or split as required to cover the space. To make a more unusual screen, cut the bottom edge into scallops or use one strip as a tie-back. Another variation on the theme of door screens is the bead curtain, which comes in several materials including wood and plastic. These can be rigged up with the minimum of fuss, and are very effective for screening an opening without robbing it of daylight.

with split pins. Use thick, hairy twine to roll up some of the screens and seawashed pebbles to weight the ties. This witty, elegant and, above all, cheap design can also be used to screen windows.

Another very effective screen or blind can be made from corrugated cardboard. Trim a roll of natural-coloured cardboard slightly wider than the window recess. Unroll the cardboard and tape, glue or staple one end to a wooden pole. Screw a large cup hook or decorative bolt into the frame at either side of the window, and set the pole on top. Drape long cotton tapes over the pole to fall behind and in front of the cardboard, which can then be neatly rolled up and secured by tying the tapes in a bow. The screen can be raised and lowered as desired, and is sturdy enough to last well. This idea also works well as a door screen. More permanent effects can be achieved by using corrugated plastic.

A temporary screen can be made very quickly from a lace-edged tablecloth or shawl. Drape it over the top of an open sash window

Above: Create your own desert island by hanging humble beach mats around a four-poster bed. Continue the theme by suspending seashore pebbles from the ends of the ties.
Right: Extend the summer by arranging a line of sunflowers along a windowsill. Tall flowers make ideal screening devices and the artificial varieties are just as effective as the real thing.

Screens – room by room

Heraldic dining-room screen

The fleur-de-lis fabric covering this screen and the fat golden tassels draped between the panels suggest both the medieval and the French Empire style. The wrong side of the fabric gives a mirror image of the right side; this feature has been exploited here with the middle panel covered in the reversed design.

The rich appearance of the screen makes it perfect for a dining room decorated in rich colours, with candelabras to provide flickering candlelight. A sitting room with ornate gilt frames and velvet drapes would also provide a good setting.

You will need

- Pre-cut three-panel screen
- Mediumweight polyester or cotton wadding
- Thin black felt-tip pen
- Scissors
- Glue brush
- PVA glue
- Furnishing fabric
- Protective goggles
- Staple gun
- Narrow petersham ribbon
- Two piano hinges
- Screwdriver
- Two pairs of large gold tassels

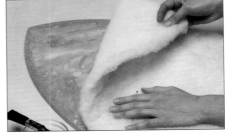

1 Lay one panel on the wadding and draw carefully around it three times. Cut out the wadding shapes and glue one to the front of each panel, using PVA glue. Leave to dry.

2 Cut two pieces of fabric for each panel, each 5 cm (2 in) larger than the panel all round. Wearing protective goggles, drape a piece of fabric over one side of each panel and staple in place, pulling the fabric taut and working from side to side towards the corners.

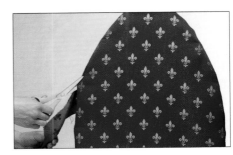

3 Trim the excess fabric back to 3 mm (⅛ in) from the staples. Cover the backs of the panels with fabric, turning under the raw edges. Glue the petersham ribbon around the sides to neaten the edges. Hinge the panels together. Drape the tassels over the screen.

Gold-and-silver living room **screen**

This screen could not be simpler to make, yet it will give a feeling of oriental elegance to any living room, traditional or modern. Silver and gold squares are cut from Chinese "spirit money", which is placed in the tombs of the dead to represent real money. You could also use brightly coloured paper and paint for a hot, mosaic effect.

You will need

- Pre-cut three-panel screen
- Water-based wood undercoat
- Paintbrush
- Protective face mask
- Fine sandpaper
- Gold acrylic paint
- Scissors
- Spirit money (see Suppliers)
- PVA glue
- Two piano hinges
- Screwdriver

1 *Apply two coats of undercoat to each panel. Wearing a protective face mask, lightly sand each panel between coats. Paint each panel with two coats of gold acrylic paint.*

2 *Carefully cut gold and silver squares from the spirit money, leaving a small white border around each.*

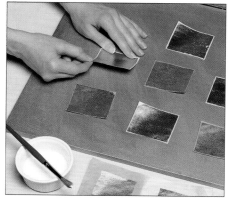

3 *Arrange the squares on the panels. When you are satisfied with the design, stick the spirit money in position using PVA glue. Hinge the panels together.*

Blackboard kitchen **screen**

This is the perfect screen for every jaded city-dweller who dreams of running a little country *auberge* – a blackboard where soup of the day and à la carte menus can be chalked up, whetting family and guests' appetites. You could even add a small shelf to hold chalk and a duster.

You will need

- Pre-cut three-panel screen
- oil-based wood undercoat
- Paintbrush
- Protective face mask
- Fine sandpaper
- Satin-finish oil-based paint
- Ruler
- Masking tape
- Scissors
- Blackboard paint
- Two piano hinges
- Screwdriver

1 *Apply two coats of undercoat to each panel. Wearing a protective face mask, lightly sand the panels between each coat. When the undercoat has dried, apply two coats of oil-based paint and leave to dry.*

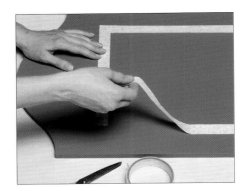

2 *Measure out the area of your blackboard on the panel, then mark out with masking tape.*

3 *Fill in the masked-off areas with blackboard paint. Leave the paint to dry, then add another coat if necessary. Leave to dry and carefully peel away the masking tape. Hinge the panels together.*

Chicken-wire kitchen **screen**

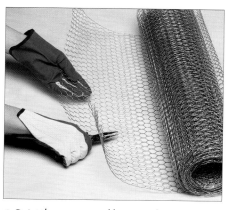

1 Paint the screen and leave to dry. Wearing protective gloves, cut lengths of chicken wire slightly larger than each frame of the screen.

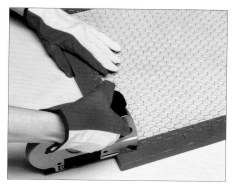

2 Place a piece of chicken wire on the back of each frame. Gently push the edges of the wire flat against the frame and then, wearing protective goggles, staple in position.

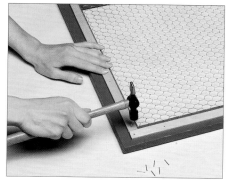

3 Place lengths of wooden battening over the cut edges of the chicken wire and fix in position with panel pins using the tack hammer. Paint the strips the same colour as the frames. Hinge the panels together.

This unusual kitchen screen is attractively rustic, and useful too. All sorts of lightweight utensils, aprons, tea towels, bunches of dried herbs and strings of garlic and chillies can be suspended from the mesh panels, using metal hooks or lengths of string. At the same time, the screen will cleverly hide waste bins and kitchen clutter from view.

You will need

- Open-panel screen (unhinged)
- Satin-finish oil-based paint
- Paintbrush
- Protective gloves
- Chicken wire
- Pliers or wire-cutters
- Protective goggles
- Staple gun
- Wooden battening
- Panel pins
- Tack hammer
- Two pairs of hinges
- Screwdriver

Perspex bathroom **screen**

A folding screen is the perfect bathing accessory, especially if you have a draughty or cavernous bathroom. This screen is inspired by the etched-glass windows that were a feature of Victorian and Edwardian homes. It is very simple to achieve a similar effect with stencils on Perspex panels.

You will need

- Roll of sticky-backed plastic
- Pen
- Scissors
- Perspex panels
- White enamel spray paint
- Protective face mask
- Protective gloves
- Clamps
- Workbench
- Drill
- Perspex cement and applicator
- Painted open-panel screen (unhinged)
- Screws
- Screwdriver
- Two pairs of hinges

1 Draw and cut your own stencil designs from the sticky-backed plastic. Remove the backing and position on the Perspex panels. Rub over the edges of the stencils.

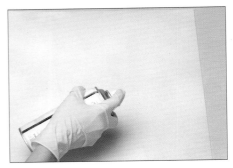

2 Shake the can of spray paint, following the manufacturer's instructions. Wearing a protective face mask and gloves, lightly spray over the stencils on to the Perspex.

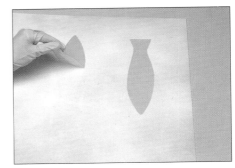

3 Leave the paint to dry, then very carefully peel off the stencils. Firmly clamp each Perspex panel and drill a hole in each corner. Spread Perspex cement around the edges of the unpainted side of the panels, and attach one to the back of each frame. When dry, screw the Perspex to the frames through the drilled holes. Hinge the panels together.

Glass-bead hall **curtain**

Handmade glass beads are perfect for screening small windows where it is impossible or impractical to have curtains. String them on to lengths of coarse parcel string and hang from a length of wooden dowel, or simply suspend them from the window frame itself. Do not worry too much about making each strand of beads the same length – they will look more interesting if they are slightly uneven.

Beads can be very heavy *en masse*, so do not use too many strands.

You will need

- Parcel string
- Scissors
- Thick wooden dowel, cut to fit the window
- Glass beads, in a variety of colours and with one larger bead per thread

1 *Cut a length of parcel string to twice the required length. Fold in half and loop over the dowel to keep it firmly in place.*

2 *Knot the two halves of the string tightly together under the loop, then cut off one half. Thread beads on to the string, tying a knot beneath each one.*

3 *When the strand is long enough, tie a large bead on the end. Make more strands to complete the curtain.*

Pierced-star bedroom **screen**

1 *Apply two coats of undercoat to each panel. Wearing a protective face mask, sand the panels between each coat. Draw a star motif on tracing paper. Place the tracing face down on each panel, making sure that it is centred, and redraw over the lines.*

2 *Using a ruler and pencil, divide the edges of the star into 2 cm (¾ in) lengths. Make a mark at the centre of each star.*

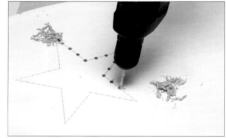

3 *Place each panel on a drilling board and clamp it firmly to a workbench. Carefully drill holes around the star, stopping as you reach the drilling board each time. Use a rolled-up piece of sandpaper to neaten the edges of the holes, then apply two coats of emulsion paint using a different colour for each panel. Allow to dry, then seal the panels with two coats of varnish. Hammer in the brass upholstery tacks and hinge the panels together.*

Pierced wooden room dividers are a common sight in India and North Africa. Here, the panels are painted in hot, earthy colours and are simply drilled with a star motif. Circles, hearts or stylized flowers would look just as good. The edges of each panel are embellished with brass upholstery tacks for extra richness.

You will need

- Pre-cut three-panel screen
- Water-based wood undercoat
- Paintbrush
- Protective face mask
- Fine sandpaper
- Tracing paper
- Pencil
- Ruler
- Drilling board
- Workbench
- Clamps
- Drill
- Emulsion paint in three colours
- Matt acrylic varnish
- Varnish brush
- Brass upholstery tacks
- Hammer
- Two piano hinges
- Screwdriver

Stamped twilight **screen**

Stamping is a simple way to create a very effective design with the minimum of effort – an area the size of a screen panel can be covered in just a few minutes. It is a good idea to divide the panels roughly first so that the pattern, though not perfectly precise, is more or less regular.

The dramatic twilight blue and gold colouring of this screen would create a wonderful theatrical prop for an *al fresco* evening party.

You will need

- Pre-cut three-panel screen
- Water-based wood undercoat
- Paintbrush
- Emulsion paint: light blue and dark blue
- Household sponge
- Gold acrylic paint
- Old plate or saucer
- Small foam roller
- Stamp
- Matt acrylic varnish
- Varnish brush
- Two piano hinges
- Screwdriver

1 *Undercoat each panel, then apply two coats of light blue emulsion. When dry, sponge diluted dark blue emulsion on top, creating plenty of bubbles. Leave to dry.*

2 *Squeeze some gold acrylic paint on to a plate or saucer. Using the roller, spread out the paint, then roll it over the stamp's surface.*

3 *Position the stamp on a panel and press down lightly, taking care not to smudge the paint. Lift the stamp straight off without twisting it. Repeat on each panel. Seal the panels with two coats of acrylic varnish. When dry, hinge the panels together.*

Outdoor **screens**

Screens can be just as attractive outdoors as they are in the home, with the added bonus that they can be growing, living structures as well as man-made. One of the beauties of having a garden, yard or patio, whatever its size, is that it is your own private, personal piece of the outdoors to relax in without interruption. However, if you are overlooked by neighbours or have no shelter from the elements, you may yearn for an enclosed area or a secret den. These are easy to create with plants and structures such as trellises or dividers.

One of the easiest ways to provide screening is to grow rows of tall flowers such as hollyhocks, foxgloves and – the ultimate giant – the sunflower. Their height creates a visual divide between separate areas and hides ugly fences and walls; when fully grown, they also provide welcome shade on hot summer days. For a splash of Mediterranean style, pot up large numbers of one plant – for example, geraniums – in single earthenware

flowerpots, then arrange them in long rows up and down steps, or pile high on wooden shelving around a yard or patio.

Wooden trellises are good for increasing the height of a dividing wall between gardens without blocking too much light. Train climbing plants such as clematis over the trellis to produce a luscious growing screen, providing colour and privacy. Trellises are also perfect for making "walls" if you wish to produce a more enclosed space in the garden, for example to screen an eating area and give shelter from evening breezes. They can also be extended overhead to form a small "room", providing a shady retreat in a quiet corner.

A robust and very stylish alternative to trellising is wattle fencing. This comes in panels, or hurdles, of densely woven wood such as willow or hazel, and is very strong and virtually impenetrable. Wattle fences were once used to divide fields and

Above: *Hide dustbins from view with a stylish stripy windbreak. Intended for the beach, a windbreak adds a splash of colour to the garden while acting as an effective screening device.*

Left: *A cotton sheet or a crisp checked tablecloth provides welcome relief from the hot sun or cool breezes while you enjoy some al fresco relaxation. Simply peg it to a washing line to make a simple screen.*

make houses, and they have been in evidence in Europe since the Iron Age. The hurdles can be lashed together and used as a portable screen, providing a windbreak or shelter in an open space. Alternatively, you can root them permanently in the ground in the same way as a trellis, to support climbing plants.

Cotton sheets pegged on a washing line are the perfect example of everyday objects providing inspiration for impromptu screening. This idea can be used to create a sheltered picnic spot in a corner of the garden, giving protection from intense sunlight and cool breezes. Run a line of cord between two trees and simply drape a sheet, duvet cover, light blanket or tablecloth over it. If there is a breeze, keep the fabric in place with a few clothes pegs.

Above: *Wooden trellising or rustic wattle hurdles can be used to create small outdoor "rooms", to add height to existing fences, or simply to provide a windbreak against late summer breezes.*

Unsightly dustbins are always a problem, especially if your outside space is small. You can place tall, bushy shrubs in containers around bins to screen them from view – these are easy to move when the bins are emptied. Another solution is a windbreak. These are generally used to provide shelter on the beach but they are perfect for concealing a multitude of things, including bins. Widely available in the summer season, their striped panels come in a huge range of colours, from subtle pastels to bright primaries.

Opulent and Grand

Sumptuous, heavy drapes worthy of a medieval castle, seductively shimmering metal leaf, plush velvet ribbons and jewel-like painted silk all make bold, striking room dividers and screens. The dramatic impact of this type of screen can be enormous, adding a touch of theatrical grandeur to the most neutral décor. The materials used are all easily obtainable and with just a lick of emulsion paint, paper stencils, metallic marker pens and richly coloured fabrics, your room can take on an air of opulent finery reminiscent of a Byzantine palace.

Gallery

Ever since the 17th and 18th centuries, when the oriental style was so popular, there have been screens of great opulence and grandeur. They have always been a vehicle for whatever furnishing style happened to be in vogue at the time. Screens are hugely versatile blank canvases, and every historical style from Empire to Gothic to neo-classical has been used to decorate them.

The screens featured here all make striking design statements – they include animal-print fabric, hand-printed silk and panels cut into bold curves. They are a mine of inspiration, showing just how dramatic large-scale fabric and paint effects can be.

Right: *The arched panels of this large, richly coloured screen give it a Gothic appearance. Inspired by architecture, especially that of Antoni Gaudi in Barcelona, it has a slightly quirky centre of gravity that makes it all the more dramatic. Multiple layers of torn hand-coloured paper have been applied to each panel, creating a rich opulence that is further enhanced by extravagant swirls of gold.*

Juliet Helen Walker

Left: *The wonderfully ornate motifs covering the panels of this screen were inspired by Byzantine decoration. The patterns have been hand-printed on to subtly shiny viscose velvet, using discharge dyes. These dyes displace the pigment in the fabric, leaving a negative mark. The patterns vary according to which way up the velvet is used.*

Anne Toomey

Right: *This screen's framework is made from steel, twisted into decorative curlicues at top and bottom. The panel is made from heavy silk dupion – hand-painted, stencilled and finally printed in rich, glowing colours.*
Neil Bottle

Left: *This fantastically shaped screen combines chinoiserie, rococo and sheer exuberance all in one. The panels are painstakingly cut from wood and then découpaged with torn paper that has been stained with oil paints and inks. Further applications of paint combine to give a surface that resembles marble. The curves of the panels are emphasized with curlicues of gold paint.*

Juliet Helen Walker

Left: *Animal-print fabrics always evoke a sensual, luxurious atmosphere, and this sumptuous screen is no exception. The exotic fabric is enhanced by the bright mesh set into each panel.*

Tessa Brown

Opposite: *The faded grandeur of these dividers, with their enigmatic decorations, is achieved with a mixture of processes – including hand printing, dyeing, transfer printing and embroidery. The base of the dividers is made from antique fabric, carefully selected and embellished with illustrated panels.*

Natasha Kerr

Gilded
screen

This richly coloured, ornate screen has been embellished with gold Dutch metal leaf, which is a cheaper alternative to true gold leaf. The technique of gilding may at first seem rather daunting, but is quite straightforward if you use ready-mixed gold size and follow these steps closely. Gilding materials can be obtained from good art suppliers or craft shops; Dutch metal leaf comes in a variety of types and colours and can be found in specialist shops or direct by mail order. Copy the stencils from the back of the book, or experiment with your own designs.

You will need

- Pre-cut three-panel screen
- Water-based wood undercoat
- Paintbrush
- Emulsion paint: dark green and red
- Ruler
- Pencil
- Gilt cream
- White spirit
- Small bowl
- Soft cloth
- Stencil film
- Craft knife
- Cutting mat
- Stencil brush or paintbrush with squared-off bristles
- Japanese gold size
- Gold Dutch metal leaf
- Silver marker pen
- Two piano hinges
- Screwdriver

1 Undercoat the panels, then apply two coats of dark green emulsion. Draw a border around each panel 2 cm (¾ in) from the edge. Draw a second border inside the first, 15 cm (6 in) from the edge. Dilute the gilt cream 50/50 with white spirit and apply to the area between the pencil lines, using a paintbrush. Leave to dry for 4–6 hours, then buff with a soft cloth.

2 Cut the stencil design from a sheet of stencil film, using a craft knife and cutting mat. Draw a line 8 cm (3 in) from the edge of the panels. Place the centre of the stencil on this line, and stipple red paint through the cut-out areas to transfer the design. Leave to dry.

3 Working in a well-ventilated area, place the stencil over the painted areas again and stipple through a coat of gold size. Leave the size to dry for about 30 minutes until it feels tacky.

4 Lay the metal leaf face down on top of the sized areas. Rub over the backing paper with a dry brush. Peel away the backing. Once all the gold leaf is applied, dust away any excess. Using a silver pen, outline the design and add shadows. Hinge the panels together.

Printed and painted
room divider

This bold room divider has been made of painted and printed cloth. Its scale makes it perfect for partitioning a larger-than-average room, such as a warehouse loft, and it would also be ideal for screening an oversize window. The basic design is applied with a silk screen. Stencils are used to mask out parts of the screen before paint is pulled through, leaving an image behind on the fabric. If you have never tried this technique before, practise on some scraps of fabric first.

You will need

- Paper
- Pencil
- Cutting mat
- Craft knife
- Old blanket
- Plastic sheet

- Masking tape
- Pre-shrunk unbleached calico, cut into three panels
- Water-based, iron-fixable fabric paints in various colours, including black
- Paintbrush
- Silk screen

- Squeegee
- Artist's paintbrush
- Iron
- Cotton lining fabric
- Scissors
- Dressmaker's pins
- Needle and thread

1 Draw the design for each separate stencil on a sheet of paper. Place the paper on a cutting mat and cut out the designs, using a craft knife.

2 Cover your work surface with the blanket, then lay the plastic on top. Tape each calico panel in turn to the work surface, pulling the fabric taut. Paint with the background colour.

3 Position the stencils on the fabric and lay the screen over one stencil. Spread fabric paint at the top of the screen, so that there is a wide enough band of paint to cover all of the cut part of the stencil. Place the squeegee in the paint. Holding the screen firmly with one hand, pull the squeegee down the screen to print through the stencil.

➤

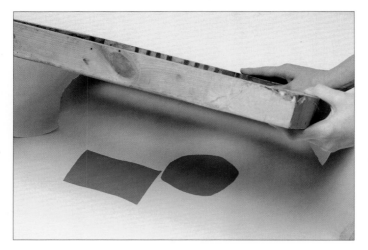

4 *Remove the squeegee and carefully lift the screen from the fabric. Peel the stencil off the back, then wash the screen and squeegee thoroughly before the paint dries. Print the other stencils in the same way, washing the screen and squeegee between colours.*

5 *When you have printed all the stencils, emphasize parts of the design by applying fabric paint freehand with the artist's paintbrush.*

6 *Finish and emphasize the design by outlining selected parts of it with black fabric paint.*

7 *Following the manufacturer's instructions, fix the paints by ironing the fabric.*

8 *Place each panel face down and press back the raw edges. Cut the lining fabric to the same dimensions, adding 2.5 cm (1 in) seam and hem allowances. Turn under the raw edges and pin to the back of each panel. Slip stitch the lining to the panels.*

Velvet-and-gold
screen

Rich fabrics exude an air of luxury and, teamed with gold, the effect is magnificent. Such grandeur could be overpowering, but with a simple motif the result is fresh and contemporary. Three slightly different shades of red velvet have been used to cover the screen, creating a subtle variation in hue. The texture of the velvet can also be distinctively altered, giving it a glossy sheen, by ironing the fabric on the back to flatten the pile. Always make sure you ventilate the room you are working in properly when using fabric paints.

You will need

- Pre-cut three-panel screen
- Silk-rayon velvet, in three slightly different shades of red
- Scissors
- Old blanket
- Plastic sheet
- Masking tape
- Tailor's chalk
- Water-based, iron-fixable gold fabric paint
- Paintbrush
- Iron
- Protective goggles
- Staple gun
- Ruler or tape measure
- Petersham ribbon
- PVA glue
- Glue brush
- Two piano hinges
- Screwdriver

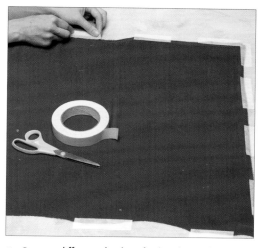

1 *Cut two different shades of velvet for each screen panel, leaving a generous margin on all sides. Cover your work surface with the blanket and tape the plastic on top. Stretch the velvet panels taut and then tape them right side up to the work surface, keeping the grain of the fabric straight.*

2 *Using tailor's chalk, draw ovals on the velvet. Draw some ovals so that they disappear off the sides of the panels to create an interesting variation in the pattern.*

3 *Fill in the ovals with gold fabric paint. Do not load the brush too heavily, as the paint spreads well and the effect is enhanced by having slightly broken colour rather than one solid block.*

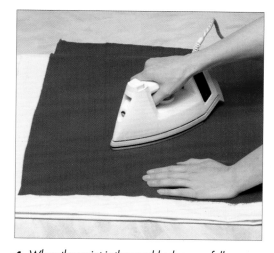

4 *When the paint is thoroughly dry, carefully untape the velvet panels. Following the manufacturer's instructions, iron each panel on the back to fix the paint.*

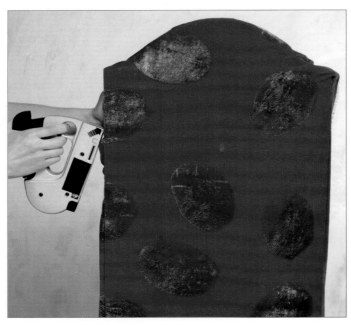

5 *Wearing protective goggles, staple a painted length of velvet to the front and back of each screen panel and rest, pulling the fabric taut and working from side to side towards the corners.*

6 *Measure around the top, one side and the bottom of a side panel. Cut two pieces of petersham ribbon to the same length, plus 6 cm (2¼ in). Cut two lengths of ribbon for the top and bottom edges of the centre panel. Spread glue along the edges of the panels and press the ribbon in place, turning under the ends. Hinge the panels together.*

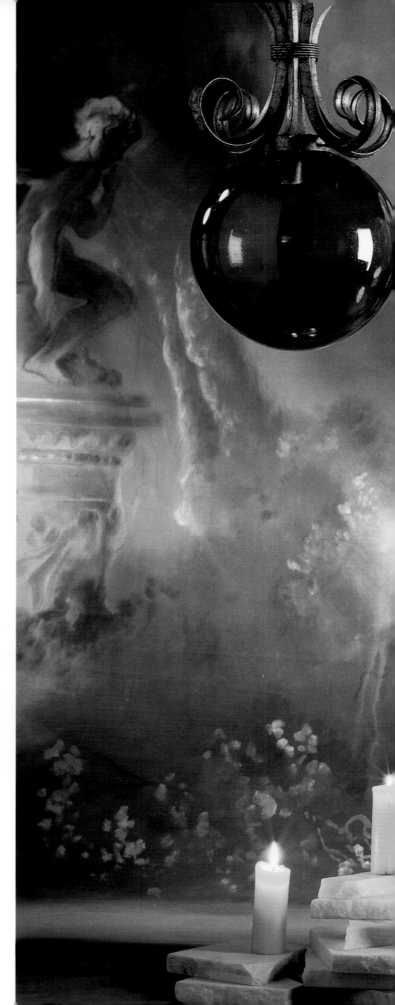

Trompe-l'oeil
screen

These flat screen panels have been painted with classical columns to create a three-dimensional optical illusion, known as *trompe l'oeil*. The rather austere and regular design has been softened by a coat of creamy water-based paint applied with a humble household sponge – the holes in the sponge create an irregular marbled effect. Finally, highlights have been added with off-white paint to emphasize the realistic result. Keep your chosen colour scheme fairly neutral, and harmonize hues for maximum effect.

You will need

- Pre-cut three-panel screen
- Water-based wood undercoat
- Paintbrush
- Emulsion paint: beige, blue-grey and off-white
- Ruler
- Pencil
- Artist's paintbrush
- Container for mixing
- Household sponge
- Matt acrylic varnish
- Varnish brush
- Two piano hinges
- Screwdriver

1 *Undercoat each panel and apply two coats of beige emulsion paint. For the columns on either side of each panel, draw pencil lines running from top to bottom, 1 cm (½ in) and 9 cm (3½ in) from the edges. Draw an 8 x 10 cm (3¼ x 4 in) rectangle at the top and bottom of each column. Divide each column into 5 cm (2 in) sections. Draw gently curving diagonal lines to join the sections from side to side, to resemble a barley twist.*

2 *Draw ovals in the centres of the rectangles at either end of each column. Draw narrow borders above and below the ovals. Draw two panels between each pair of columns, 13 cm (5 in) from either edge. The lower panel starts 10 cm (4 in) from the lower edge and is 40 cm (16 in) high. The upper panel starts 10 cm (4 in) above the lower and follows the curve of the screen at the top.*

3 *Paint along all the pencil lines, using blue-grey emulsion and the artist's paintbrush. Paint a thick line below each twist in the columns to give an illusion of depth.*

4 *Sponge diluted pale beige paint over the whole surface of each screen panel. When dry, paint off-white highlights on the columns and central panels. Seal the whole design with a coat of matt acrylic varnish, then hinge the panels together.*

Crisscross padded
screen

This richly indulgent screen has been created from sumptuous taffeta, velvet ribbon and diamanté. The screen can be put to best use in the bedroom to create a boudoir effect, providing a small oasis of luxury in a corner of the room. Each panel has been lightly padded with a mediumweight wadding that makes the fabric lie more smoothly and gives a soft, upholstered feel in keeping with its intended location.

You will need

- Mediumweight polyester or cotton wadding
- Pre-cut three-panel screen
- Felt-tip pen
- Scissors
- PVA glue
- Glue brush
- Taffeta
- Protective goggles
- Staple gun
- Dressmaker's pins
- Ruler or tape measure
- Velvet ribbon
- Diamanté pieces
- Petersham ribbon
- Two piano hinges
- Screwdriver

1 Lay the wadding on a flat surface. Place one of the screen panels on the wadding, draw around it and cut out. Cut two pieces of wadding for each panel. Glue the wadding to both sides of the panels and leave to dry.

2 Cut two pieces of taffeta 3 cm (1¼ in) larger all round for each panel. Staple one piece to each panel (see General techniques), then trim the fabric back to within 3 mm (⅛ in) of the staples. Attach the second piece to the other side of each panel, using pins to hold it in place. Turn under the edges so that they overlap the raw edges of the first piece and staple.

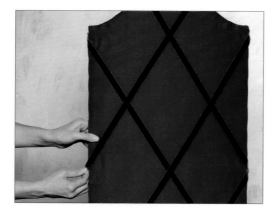

3 Place a pin at the centre bottom of each panel. Measure 30 cm (12 in) intervals up the sides. Cut two pieces of velvet ribbon to run from the centre bottom to the first pins at right and left, plus 3 cm (1¼ in). Turn under the ends and pin in place. Repeat with two lengths of ribbon from the corners to the second point, the first point to the third, and the second point to the top edges. Staple the ribbon ends in place.

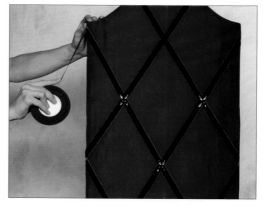

4 Glue the diamanté where the ribbons cross. Measure around the top, one side and bottom of a side panel, and cut two pieces of petersham ribbon plus 6 cm (2¼ in). Cut two pieces to fit along the top and bottom edges of the centre panel. Spread a line of glue along the edges of each panel and press the ribbon in place, turning under the ends. When the glue is dry, hinge the panels together.

Painted-silk
room divider

What could be more luxurious than a room divider made from hand-painted silk? The delicate fabric moves gently in the softest breeze. The stylized motifs are derived from Indian Mogul architectural features such as doors and arched windows. Extra richness is added with gold "gutta", a liquid which acts as a barrier and stops the paints from running together.

You will need

- 4.3 m (4¾ yd) of 115 cm (45 in) wide medium or heavyweight habutai silk
- Tape measure
- Scissors
- Iron
- Silk-painting frame
- Fine map pins
- Ruler
- Vanishing fabric marker
- Pencil and paper (optional)
- Heavy plastic sheet
- Masking tape
- Water-based gold gutta and applicator
- Containers for mixing
- Water-based, iron-fixable silk paints
- Paintbrushes
- Needle and matching thread
- Gold cord
- Dressmaker's pins
- Three small gold tassels

1 *Cut two silk panels 115 x 215 cm (45 x 85 in). Iron each panel and stretch the first over the frame, using fine map pins. Pin the silk from side to side, working across the frame, so that the grain is straight and the fabric is taut.*

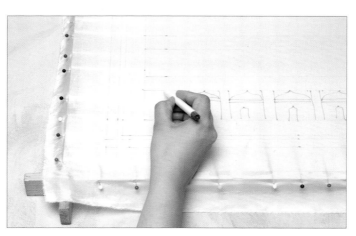

2 *Using a ruler and vanishing fabric marker, draw the borders and design on the silk. You may wish to draw your design on paper first for reference.*

➤

3 Tape the plastic to your work surface. Draw over the lines of the design with gold gutta. Turn over the screen to make sure that the gutta has penetrated through the silk. If there are gaps in the lines, add more gutta to the back of the fabric.

4 When the gutta has dried, mix the paint colours, ensuring that you have enough of each, and start to fill in the solid areas of the design. If you dot a little paint in the centre of each area of the pattern, the colour will quickly spread as far as the gutta lines.

5 Apply washes of colour around the details to fill in the background and borders. When the paint is completely dry, unpin the silk from the frame. Following the paint manufacturer's instructions, iron the silk on the back to fix the colours. Paint the second panel.

6 Handsew the panels together using small, neat stitches. Cut a length of gold cord to fit around the edge. Pin and slip stitch in position. Stitch the gold tassels to the lower edge of the fabric.

Patchwork
room divider

The subdued tones of these rich velvet curtains make them perfect for dividing off a sleeping area. Since the Middle Ages, tapestries and wall hangings have been used to screen beds, so you will be continuing a centuries-old tradition. Plan the patchwork design on squared paper, in such a way that you can make it up in horizontal strips. The curtains are quite heavy, so suspend them from a strong wooden or cast-iron pole. A design of large diamonds set in rectangles is used here, based on one triangular template.

You will need

- Tape measure
- Squared graph paper
- Felt-tip pen
- Ruler
- Thin card
- Paper scissors
- Velvet, in various toning colours
- Pinking shears
- Dressmaker's pins
- Tacking thread and needle
- Sewing machine
- Matching thread
- Iron
- Curtain weights (optional)
- Lining fabric
- Tailor's chalk

1 *Calculate the desired size of each curtain, and draw a scaled-down version on squared paper. Draw and cut full-size card templates adding a 1 cm (½ in) seam allowance all around. Draw around the templates on to the back of the velvet, and cut out with pinking shears.*

2 *The patchwork is made up in horizontal strips. Pin, tack and machine pairs of triangles together to make rectangles, then join these together. Press the seams open and then join the strips together to make each curtain, carefully matching intersection points. Trim the seam allowances.*

3 *Calculate how many loops you need for the top of each curtain, allowing 12–15 cm (5–6 in) between each. For each loop, cut a rectangle of velvet 20 x 32 cm (8 x 12½ in). With right sides together, fold in half lengthways and stitch the long edge. Position the seam in the centre of the loop, press the seam open and turn the loop right side out. Fold the loops in half and tack into position.*

4 *Cut a velvet facing for the top of each curtain 10 cm (4 in) deep. Pin and tack over the raw edges of the loops, then stitch the top and side edges. Clip the corners and turn the facing right side out. Make a facing for the bottom in the same way, but stitch the bottom and side seams. Press under a 1 cm (½ in) turning on the sides.*

➤

5 *Attach the top and bottom facings, using herringbone stitch and inserting curtain weights if required. Cut a piece of lining fabric the same width as each curtain and 14 cm (5½ in) shorter. Turn under a 1 cm (½ in) hem along the side edges and press.*

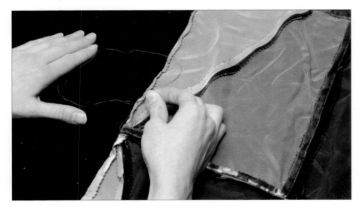

6 *Using tailor's chalk, mark a central line down the wrong side of each lining piece. Mark parallel lines at 30 cm (12 in) intervals on either side of the line. Pin each curtain and lining together at the central line. Fold the fabric back over the pins and lock stitch the two together. Repeat at each marked line across each curtain.*

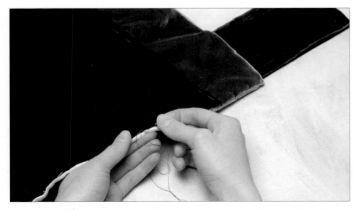

7 *Turn under the raw edges all the way around each lining, then slip stitch the lining to the curtain along each edge.*

Byzantine screen

Rich, classic colours and a liberal application of gold give this screen an image of opulent splendour. Position the screen in a formal setting, surrounded with velvet drapes, dark furniture and metal candlesticks to complete the effect.

Although seemingly quite complex, the decoration is very easy to apply using a gold pen and ruler – the most important aspect is to measure and mark out the design accurately before you start work. Draw the design at full size on a large sheet of paper first, if wished.

You will need

- Pre-cut three-panel screen
- Water-based wood undercoat
- Paintbrush
- Emulsion paint: rich red and French blue
- Ruler
- Pencil
- Gold paint
- Artist's paintbrush
- Gold marker pen with medium nib
- Two piano hinges
- Screwdriver

1 Undercoat the panels, then apply two coats of red emulsion. Draw a border around the front of each panel 2 cm (¾ in) from the edge. Add a second border 6 cm (2¼ in) from the edge. Draw a third border 8 cm (3 in) from the edge.

2 Paint lines of gold dots around the outside of each panel. Add a second row of dots between the second and third pencil lines.

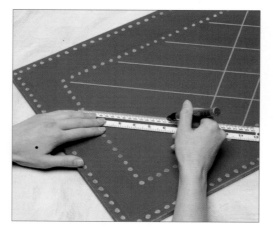

3 Mark four points at equal distances along the bottom of the inner border, then at the same distance apart around the rest of the border. Starting in the bottom lefthand corner, draw a line to the third point on the righthand side, using the gold pen. Continue in the same way until all the marks are joined. Then draw lines from right to left, to make a trellis pattern.

4 Draw over the border lines, using the gold pen. Then paint a thin blue line on the inside of the borders and on either side of the diagonal lines. Draw gold stars where the diagonal lines intersect and add a dot of blue to the centre of each star. Hinge the panels together.

Organic and Natural

W̶HETHER YOU LIKE
CLEAN LINES AND
COOL, NEUTRAL TONES
OR YOU PREFER LEAVES, TWIGS AND THE
FRUITS OF THE FOREST, NATURE
PROVIDES A HUGE VARIETY OF COLOURS,
SHAPES AND DESIGNS TO FIRE THE
IMAGINATION. COMBINE LEAF
SKELETONS WITH DELICATE HANDMADE
PAPER TO MAKE AN ELEGANT ROOM
DIVIDER, OR EXPERIMENT WITH
SEASHELLS AND EARS OF CORN TO ADD
AN AURA OF TRANQUILLITY TO A
FOLDING SCREEN. ROSE PETALS AND
SEPIA PHOTOGRAPHS GIVE A NOSTALGIC
GLIMPSE OF THE PAST, AND LEAF, MOSS
AND TWIG SCREENS CONJURE UP
MEMORIES OF COUNTRY WALKS.

Gallery

There are so many ways you can use natural materials to make unusual screens and room dividers. Unbleached muslin, hessian, leaves, seed pods, flower heads, bark, Japanese paper, shells and driftwood, supple twigs and natural cord – all these are worth collecting and preserving, and all can be incorporated into a screen.

The beauty of natural materials is their abstract, slightly mysterious quality. Some of the screens shown here look as though they evolved spontaneously, others as if they were assembled from a collection of found objects that were carefully preserved until the right companion pieces were discovered. In all cases, they are typified by their simple, organic forms.

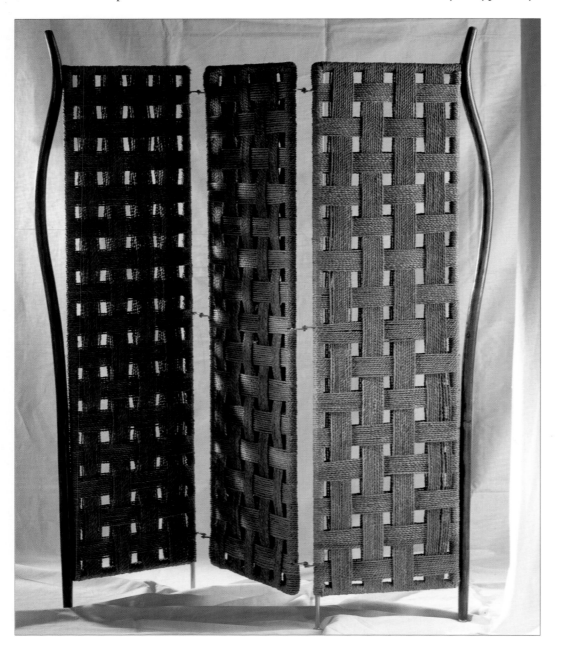

Left: *This elegant, warmly coloured screen with its sinuously curved legs is made from seagrass and hardwood. The seagrass was cut and then formed by hand into long, smooth cords, woven to make subtle yet sturdy panels.*

Paperchase

Opposite: *The base of this screen is linen scrim, with a plaid appearance achieved by drawing the threads. This motif is continued to the base of the panel to make a long fringe. It is decorated with a mixture of appliqué and organic objects – slices of preserved fruit, pressed pansy flowers and poppy heads. Some are glued in position, others are encased in pockets of silk chiffon.*

Sarah Feather

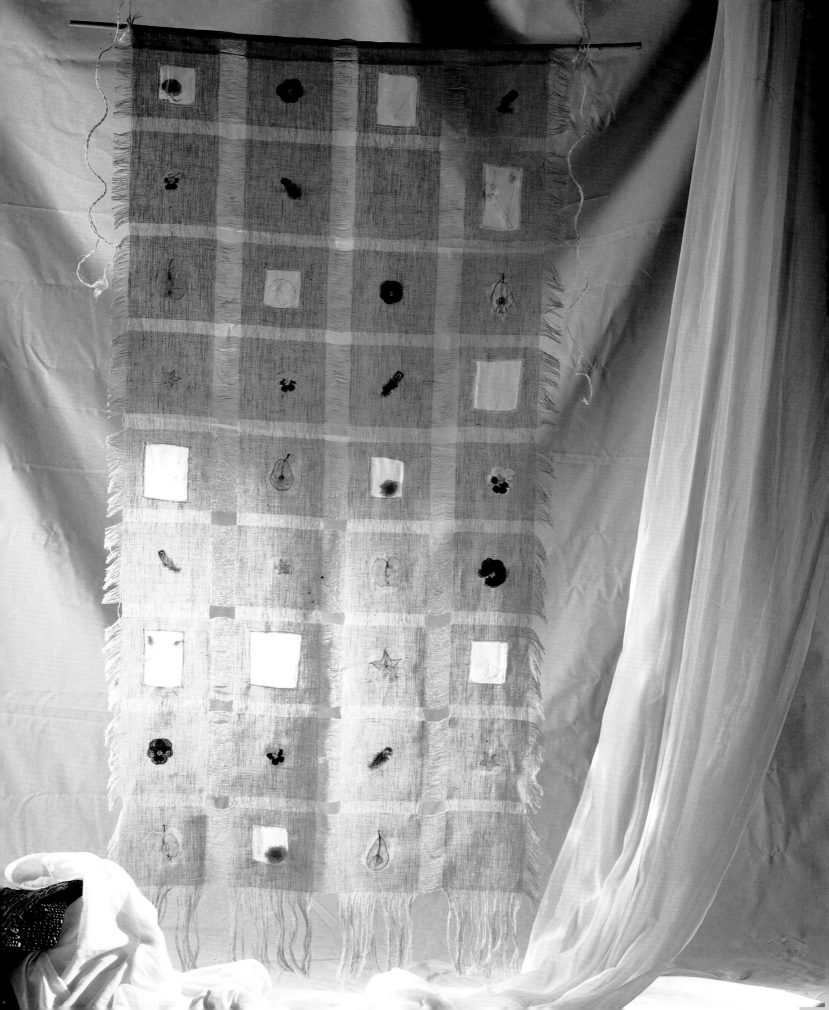

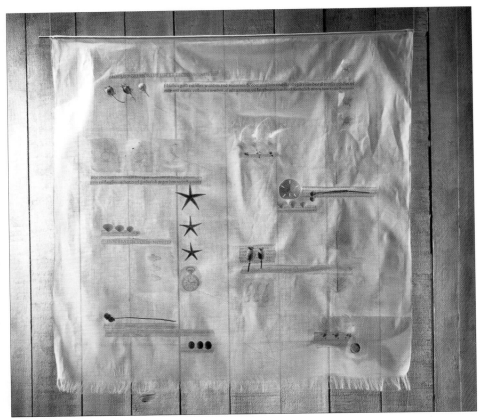

Left: *This ethereal room divider is made from frayed and stiffened muslin. It is embellished with precisely placed objects, including starfish, poppy heads, leaf skeletons, seed heads, feathers and gold inscriptions on tissue paper. Most of these are glued in place except for the feathers, which are held in position with sealing wax.*
Mandy Pritty

Below left: *The smooth bark of the thin, dark twigs contrasts with the unfinished surface of this screen's uprights. The densely structured panels only let in chinks of light.*
Paperchase

Below right: *The chunky appearance of this screen is accentuated by the rough-hewn slices of wood that run horizontally across the middle of both panels. The screen was made in the Philippines entirely from recycled wood.*
Paperchase

Left: *The black and white paper used to create this folding screen gives it a bold, clean look. The framework is made from maple wood and the paper is supported by fine aluminium rods that slot into the uprights. The rods have been carefully positioned so that they grip the paper, and it needs no other mode of fixing. The paper was rolled first and, when curved back on itself, created enough tension to keep it in place.*
Alison White

Right: *This wonderfully untamed screen is made from coppiced hazel wood. The panels were formed by weaving cleft and round rods together to make a thick, strong mesh. Coppiced hazel has been used since the earliest times. Its strength and impenetrable nature made it ideal for holding back river banks and sand dunes, and to keep flocks of sheep safely in their fields.*
Jason Griffiths

Woodland
screen

Owning this twiggy delight is like having your own portable wood to move around your home! A soft bed of moss and leaves is trapped in green chicken wire and topped by supple sprouting twigs. The screen retains a natural appearance and looks as if it is growing indoors. Use it to make a restful corner in a living room. Farmed moss is produced in an environmentally friendly way. If you gather any moss from the countryside, take a little from several places to avoid destroying entire colonies. Preserved leaves retain the suppleness of fresh leaves.

You will need

- Pre-cut two-panel screen
- PVA glue
- Glue brush
- Farmed or wood moss
- Preserved and dried leaves
- Protective goggles
- Protective gloves
- Green plastic-covered chicken wire
- Pliers or wire-cutters
- Staple gun
- Florist's wire
- Birch or willow twigs
- Two piano hinges
- Screwdriver

1 Spread PVA glue over each panel and lay pieces of moss on top, ensuring that the entire surface of each panel is covered. Leave the panels to dry.

2 Arrange the leaves on top of the moss, placing the brightly coloured ones where they will catch the eye. Wearing protective goggles and gloves, cut pieces of chicken wire to fit each panel and staple in position.

3 Trim any excess chicken wire. Cut 20 cm (8 in) lengths of florist's wire and staple them around the outside edges and top of each panel. (Leave the inside edges so that you can attach the hinges.)

4 Make 5–8 cm (2–3 in) thick bundles of twigs. Tie them tightly together using florist's wire and pliers or wire-cutters. Place the bundles against the edges of the panels and tie tightly, using the stapled lengths of wire. Curve the twigs around the top of each panel. Hinge the panels together, then attach more twigs to the middle of the screen with wire.

Floral firescreen

This gorgeous screen makes a lovely centrepiece for an empty fireplace during the summer months. Colourful dried flowers are supported in wire-and-moss bowls, and the edges of the screen are framed with supple birch twigs. The firescreen is for decoration only, and should never be placed near a lighted fire. If you gather any moss from the countryside, take a little from several places to avoid destroying entire colonies. Farmed moss is produced in an environmentally friendly way, and can be obtained from specialist suppliers and from some florists.

You will need

- Pre-cut firescreen
- Green acrylic paint
- Paintbrush
- Wood glue
- Glue brush
- PVA glue
- Farmed or wood moss
- Protective gloves
- Protective goggles
- Green plastic-coated chicken wire
- Pliers or wire-cutters
- Staple gun
- Florist's wire
- Birch or willow twigs
- Florist's foam
- Dried flowers
- Natural raffia

1 *Paint the feet of the screen with green acrylic paint and glue them in position at the base of the screen using wood glue. Spread PVA glue over the front of the screen and stick the moss in place, covering the panel completely. Leave to dry.*

2 *Wearing protective gloves and goggles, cut a piece of chicken wire large enough to cover the screen. Cut the wire to fit around the feet, then staple to the front of the screen. Trim away any excess moss and wire.*

3 *Cut 20 cm (8 in) lengths of florist's wire and staple them every 15 cm (6 in) around the top and sides of the screen.*

4 *Make 5–8 cm (2–3 in) thick bundles of twigs and tie each tightly together, using lengths of florist's wire and pliers. You will need two to fit the sides of the screen, and two to fit around the top.*

➤

5 *Place the twig bundles against the edges of the screen and bind tightly in place, using the stapled wire lengths.*

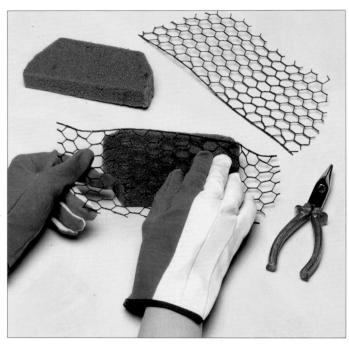

6 *Cut the florist's foam to make two bowl shapes, then cut two pieces of chicken wire and mould them to the shape of the foam. Line the wire bowls with moss, place the foam inside and staple to the centre of the screen. Trim any excess wire.*

7 *Insert the dried flowers into the foam in the top bowl one by one, to create a bouquet. Cut lengths of twig and push them into the lower bowl to make the "stems" of the flowers.*

8 *Using long lengths of raffia, tie a large, full bow and glue it to the centre of the bouquet.*

Elements
screen

The design of this screen is inspired by the elements, and shells and stalks of corn have been used as decoration. The cool blue of the "air" and "water" side panels contrasts with the warm tones of the central "earth" design. The overall effect is calming and peaceful, making the screen ideal for a bedroom or bathroom setting. The acrylic paint is applied quite thickly in horizontally graduated lines with a small palette knife, giving the panels a richly textured surface that also breaks up the colour beautifully.

You will need

- Pre-cut three-panel screen
- Water-based wood undercoat
- Paintbrush
- White emulsion paint
- Protective face mask
- Fine sandpaper
- Small palette knife
- Acrylic paint: white, blue, brown and silver
- Containers for mixing
- Star stencil
- Scallop shells
- Plaster filler
- Epoxy resin glue
- Small beached starfish
- Corn stalks
- Applicator
- Two piano hinges
- Screwdriver

1 *Apply undercoat to the panels, then apply two coats of white emulsion paint. Wearing a face mask, sand lightly between coats.*

2 *Using a palette knife, apply ridges of white acrylic paint to the lower two-thirds of each panel and leave to dry.*

3 *Mix the blue and brown acrylic paint with white. Using the palette knife, apply blue paint to the two side panels and brown paint to the central panel. Make the colour more intense towards the bottom of the panels, using colour straight from the tube.*

4 *Using silver paint, stencil a star at the centre top of each side panel and a row of stars beneath it. Using brown paint, add stars to the central panel.*

➤

5 *Using a clean palette knife, fill the scallop shells with plaster filler and leave to dry.*

6 *Glue a row of scallop shells to each side panel. Glue the starfish below them. Glue the corn stalks to the central "earth" panel. Leave to dry, then hinge the panels together.*

Vivid leaf
screen

Natural materials need not always look neutral. Here, brightly coloured handmade paper is teamed very successfully with bright green preserved leaves to make a bold statement. The natural-pine frame contrasts well with the strong colours. Preserved leaves are easy to work with and look particularly natural as they retain the suppleness of new leaves. They can be obtained from specialist suppliers and some florists. Large sheets of Japanese paper in a variety of natural and dyed shades are available from good stationers.

You will need

- Open-panel pine screen
- Thin, brightly coloured Japanese paper
- Paper scissors
- Sewing machine
- Threads to contrast with and match the paper
- Paper glue
- Preserved leaves
- Dressmaker's pins
- 12 screw eyes
- 4 mm (³⁄₁₆ in) diameter wooden dowel
- Small saw

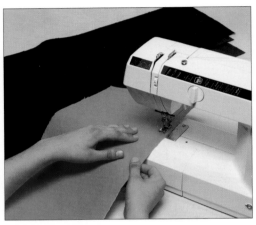

1 For the two side panels, cut one long and one short piece of paper to the same width. For the central panel, cut one long piece of paper and one slightly smaller to fit on top. Using a long stitch, machine stitch a contrasting border around each piece of paper. Make a narrow casing at the top and bottom of the panels.

2 Using paper glue, join the long and short pieces of paper to make the side panels. Glue the pieces of paper for the central panel on top of each other.

3 Pin rows of preserved leaves to the front of each panel. Using a long stitch, stitch each leaf to the paper along the central vein, removing the pins before you reach them.

4 Attach two screw eyes to the upper and lower struts of each frame. Cut six lengths of dowel to fit the pairs of screw eyes. Insert the dowels into the casings in the paper panels and then slot them into the screw eyes.

Collage
firescreen

Use old sepia photographs, sheet music and other printed ephemera to create a nostalgic firescreen full of family memories and mementoes – a future heirloom in its own right. If you do not have sufficient material of your own, you will find what you need on secondhand stalls and in junk shops. For a personal touch, dried flowers from your garden will add a subtle glow of faded colour. This screen is for decoration only, and should never be placed near a lighted fire. Keep it for the summer months or display before a disused fireplace in a bedroom or bathroom.

You will need

- Pre-cut firescreen
- Water-based wood undercoat

- Paintbrush
- White satin-finish wood paint
- Newspapers, sheet music and photographs

- PVA glue
- Glue brush
- Gold paper
- Corn stalks
- Dried rose petals

- Epoxy resin glue
- Applicator
- Masking tape
- Clear polyurethane varnish
- Varnish brush

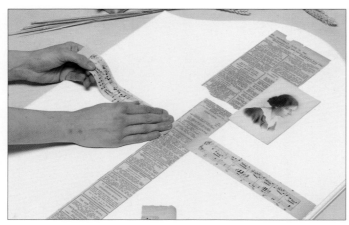

1 *Paint the firescreen and feet with two coats of undercoat and then paint all the pieces white. Tear pieces of newspaper and sheet music into strips and glue to the screen.*

2 *Lay photographs on the screen and rearrange them until you are happy with the overall design. Glue some images to rectangles of gold paper. Glue everything in position.*

3 *Using epoxy resin glue, add the corn stalks and dried rose petals. Hold the corn in place with masking tape while the glue dries.*

4 *Seal the design with a coat of varnish. Leave the firescreen to dry overnight, then slide the feet into position at the bottom.*

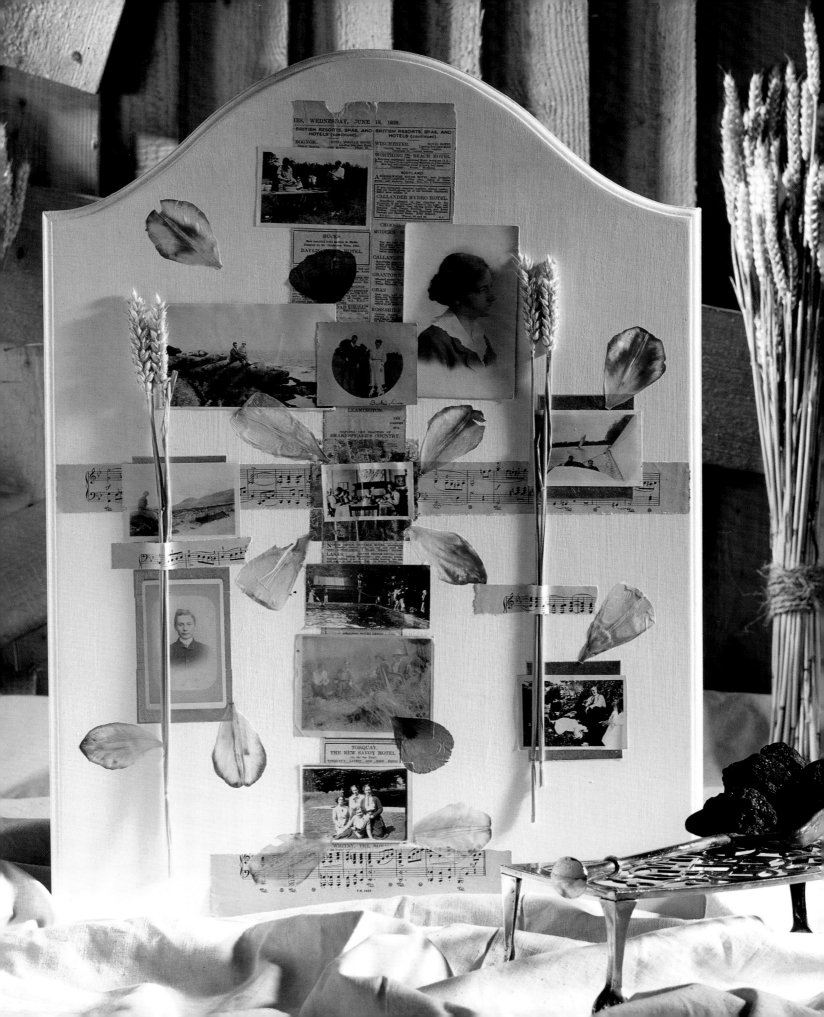

Wood and paper screen

This elegant modern firescreen is ideally suited to a contemporary minimalist setting. The paper strips are cut from rolled sheets, and the natural curl keeps the paper in position between the bands of dowel. The combined effect of the natural wood and paper and the clean, simple design is peaceful and very easy on the eye. As the paper panels are not fixed, they can be replaced with different colours.

You will need

- Six 90 cm (36 in) lengths of 5 x 2.5 cm (2 x 1 in) softwood, such as pine
- Eighteen 30 cm (12 in) lengths of 6 mm (¼ in) wooden dowel
- Protective face mask
- Fine sandpaper
- Rubber gloves
- Fine wire wool
- White emulsion paint
- Paintbrush
- Clear acrylic varnish
- Varnish brush
- Pencil
- Workbench
- Clamps
- Drill
- Wood glue
- Wooden mallet
- Two pairs of butterfly hinges
- Screwdriver
- White, heavy, textured watercolour paper
- Craft knife
- Metal ruler
- Cutting mat

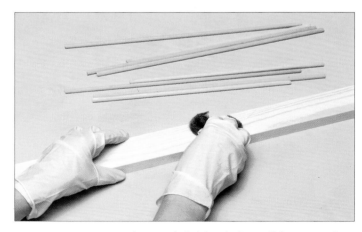

1 *Wearing a protective face mask, lightly rub down all the pieces of wood with sandpaper or wire wool. Apply a thin, patchy coat of dilute white paint to all the wood and leave it to dry. Seal the surface of each piece with varnish.*

➤

2 Mark the positions of the dowels on the inside edges of each upright. Clamp the wood firmly and carefully drill a hole about halfway though the wood at each point.

3 Glue the dowels into one half of each pair of uprights. Squeeze a little glue into the holes in the second upright of each pair and fix the two together, matching corresponding holes. Gently tap the frame halves together, using a mallet.

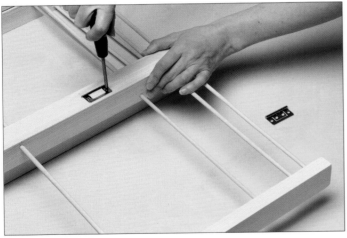

4 Place the frames side by side and mark the positions of the hinges. Make pilot holes for the screws to avoid splitting the wood, then screw the hinges in place.

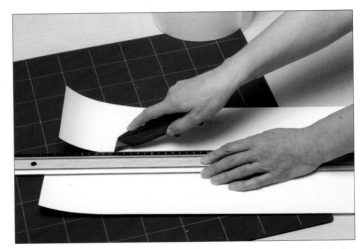

5 Cut six 12 x 90 cm (4¾ x 35½ in) lengths of paper using a craft knife, metal ruler and cutting mat. Roll the paper so that it is gently curled.

6 Weave the strips of paper in and out of the screen, experimenting to achieve the best effect.

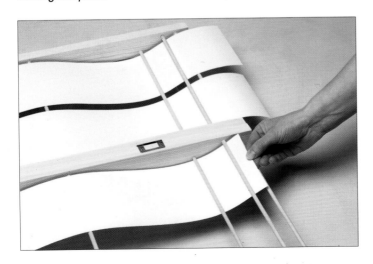

Door screen

This subtle screen makes an unusual covering for an open doorway. Squares of handmade paper are sewn to a muslin backing that is then stitched to calico. The embossed copper-foil fringe tinkles in the breeze.

The simple square motif makes a very versatile design that can be adapted to fit across a door frame of any size, or you may wish to use it simply as a decorative hanging. A multitude of handmade papers in a variety of colours and textures may be used to complement an existing décor.

You will need

- Handmade paper, in several colours
- Muslin
- Scissors
- Sewing machine
- Matching and contrasting threads
- Unbleached calico
- Dressmaker's pins
- Thin copper foil
- Sharp pencil
- Darning needle
- Sewing needle and thread
- Pliers
- Small copper jump rings
- Natural raffia

1 Tear the handmade paper into 10 cm (4 in) squares. Cut strips of muslin to the width of your door. Using a wide zigzag, stitch the squares on to the muslin, making two panels two squares deep and one panel four squares deep.

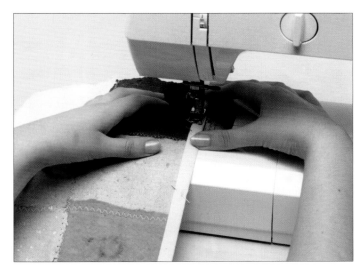

2 Cut calico strips 6 cm (2¼ in) wide and as long as the paper-and-muslin panels. Pin the calico strips along the long edges of each paper panel, turning under the raw edges. Stitch, removing the pins as you reach them.

3 Cut a piece of calico the size of the screen, plus an extra 3 cm (1¼ in) all around for turnings. Place the paper-and-muslin panels on top and turn over the raw edges of the calico, enclosing the sides of the panels. Pin and stitch the panels and the turnover in place and decorate with lines of machine embroidery. To make tabs for hanging the screen, cut strips of calico 35 x 18 cm (14 x 7 in). Fold in half lengthways, stitch and turn right side out. Fold each tube in half, turn under the raw edges and stitch at regular intervals along the top of the screen.

➤

4 Cut rectangles of copper foil. Trim any rough edges, then draw a simple design with a sharp pencil on to the back so that it is embossed on to the front. Pierce holes in the corners with a darning needle. Handstitch some of the rectangles to the centres of the paper squares.

5 Using pliers, attach the jump rings to the top corners of the remaining copper rectangles, and thread through lengths of raffia to suspend them. Sew the raffia ends to the bottom edge of the screen.

Leaf
room divider

Created from handmade Japanese *washi* paper and leaf skeletons from the sacred Bodhi tree, this delicate room divider diffuses the daylight, providing a gentle, slightly hazy retreat from bright sunshine. The divider is attached from the top edge only and, because the paper is so light, it will move softly with the slightest current of air from an open window. Leaf skeletons can be ordered from specialist suppliers and many florists.

You will need

- Leaf skeletons
- Thin Japanese *washi* paper
- Dressmaker's pins
- Sewing machine
- Matching thread

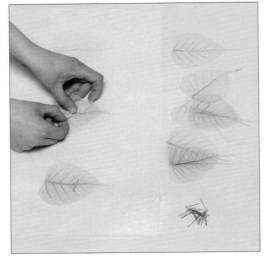

1 Pin rows of leaf skeletons to one side of a sheet of Japanese paper. Turn the paper over and pin leaves to the other side, in the same position as the first leaves.

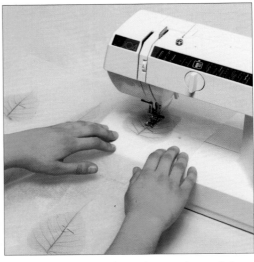

2 Using a long, straight machine stitch, attach the leaves to the paper by stitching along the line of each main vein. Remove the pins from either side of the paper before you reach them.

3 Lay two sheets of paper right sides together and machine stitch along one shorter side to join them. Continue to add more panels in the same way until the divider is the correct length. Make more long strips to fit the desired width.

4 Lay the long strips of paper right sides together so that all the seams are to the back. Stitch the long sides to complete the divider.

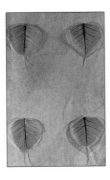

Historic and Classical

CLASSIC CRAFT TECHNIQUES SUCH AS DÉCOUPAGE HAVE ALWAYS BEEN ASSOCIATED WITH SCREEN-MAKING. LOOK TO THE DECORATIVE AND FOLK-ART TRADITIONS OF THE WORLD FOR INSPIRATION, AND YOU WILL DISCOVER ENOUGH EXCITING THEMES AND IDEAS TO DECORATE A HUNDRED SCREENS. CHOOSE BETWEEN A ROMAN MOSAIC FIRESCREEN, A SCANDINAVIAN FOLK-ART EFFECT, WONDERFULLY ORNATE PAPERCUT PANELS IN THE EASTERN EUROPEAN STYLE OR A *TROMPE-L'OEIL* FIRESCREEN.

Gallery

The screen is such a fundamental piece of furniture that most cultures have their own version. In the minimalist interiors of Japan or on the pierced verandahs of Morocco, screens play an important role in providing decorative appeal and in creating a sense of privacy and intimacy. The various shapes and styles featured here give an indication of just how versatile an object a screen can be.

The materials used differ from country to country, and one of the beauties of these screens is the different methods of manufacture employed. The sophistication of traditional découpage and cracquelure techniques contrasts strongly with the exuberance of Indian motifs, and the texture of hand-turned wooden panels contrasts with the cold finery of lacy metalwork.

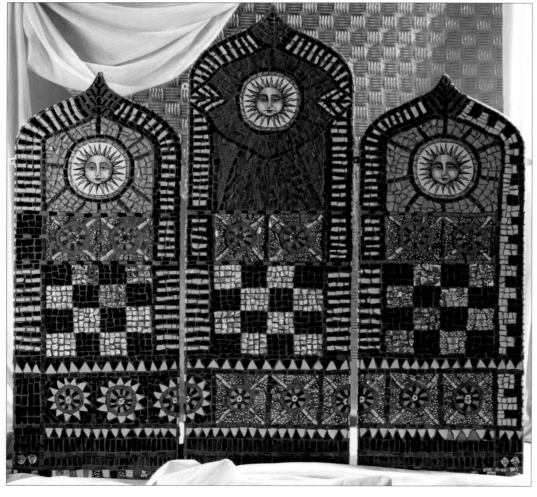

Above: *The design of leaping animals, flowers and foliage cut into this contemporary metal firescreen is derived from the large, pierced wooden room dividers traditionally found in India. The screen, which comes from northern India, was drilled and then cut with metal nippers to form the ornate pattern.*
Nice Irma's

Left: *This trio of extravagant mosaic panels is covered with fragments of broken china in scorching colours. The designs are based on Yemeni architecture and the sand paintings of Native Americans. The colours are inspired by Moorish art and architecture, and the panel borders by medal ribbons and Tibetan tiger rugs.*
Cleo Mussi

Above: *This tall, four-panelled screen was made in France in the late 19th century. Each panel is covered with tapestry, depicting a domestic interior with a group of men singing songs to a small party. The French produced many tapestry screens – indeed, the famous Savonnerie workshops made tapestry lengths specifically for screens.*

Decorative Living

Opposite: *The wrought-iron window grille is a very common architectural feature in Morocco. Here, single panels are used as partitions to screen windows. The three-panel folding screen is more unusual, although the lacy design is commonly found.*

The Kasbah

Right: *Each small section of this folding wooden screen is hand-turned in hardwood. The design is traditional and the screen is known as a "Moucharabia". It is found all over Morocco, where it is used in the home and as a screening device on verandahs.*

The Kasbah

Below: *This elegant firescreen has been skilfully treated with paint effects and specialist varnishes. A photocopied image of an old engraving was hand-coloured with diluted acrylic paint, then découpaged on to a smoky base coat. Cracquelure varnish was applied, then oil paint was rubbed into the cracks to "age" the surface.*

Paint Magic

Right: *This traditional open-panel screen is made from softwood, and has crossbars of wooden dowel through which fabric can be woven. It is designed to display removable fabric panels; this particular fabric in soft, neutral tones has been woven into an Ikat-style design.*

Tessa Brown

Scandinavian **screen**

Scandinavian style is typified by light, airy spaces, painted wood and cool colours. This screen is decorated with stylized tulips, a traditional folk-art motif that would fit well in a country-style kitchen or bedroom.

When the painted design is complete, the screen is rubbed down with coarse sandpaper to give a patchy, distressed look. It is important to sand in a vertical direction only to achieve a regular effect. Trace the tulip design from the template at the back of the book, if wished.

You will need

- Pre-cut three-panel screen
- Water-based wood
- undercoat
- Paintbrush
- Emulsion paint: beige, blue-green, red and green
- Pencil and ruler
- Tracing paper
- Thin white paper
- Artist's paintbrush
- Protective face mask
- Coarse sandpaper
- Two piano hinges
- Screwdriver

1 *Paint each panel with two coats of undercoat, allow to dry and then apply two coats of beige paint. When dry, apply a very thin coat of blue-green emulsion on top.*

2 *Mark a central area on each panel, 12 cm (5 in) in from the edges. Apply a thin coat of beige emulsion to the panel so that the blue-green background is still visible through the paint.*

3 *Trace the tulip design and transfer it to the paper. Scribble over the back. Draw a faint line down the centre of the beige panels. Place the tulip design on each panel, with the line running through the centre of the design. Draw over the design to transfer it on to the panels.*

4 *Using the artist's paintbrush, paint the tulips. Paint a red border around the beige panels and around the edges of each screen panel. Wearing a protective face mask, rub down each panel with sandpaper to reveal areas of colour. Hinge the panels together.*

Papercut
screen

This screen is inspired by traditional Polish papercuts, made at certain times of the year such as Easter to decorate farmhouse walls. Cool Scandinavian colours are used here instead of the more exuberant Polish colours. Trace the flowerpot template from the back of the book.

You will need

- Pre-cut three-panel screen
- Water-based wood primer
- Paintbrush
- Blue-grey satin-finish wood paint
- Scissors

- Thin paper: white, red, yellow and blue
- Pencil and ruler
- Pair of compasses
- Pinking shears
- Hole punch
- Fungicide-free wallpaper paste

- Container for mixing
- Glue brush
- Tracing paper
- Thin white card
- Bulldog clips
- Two piano hinges
- Screwdriver

1 Paint the screen panels with primer, then apply two coats of blue-grey paint. Also paint the edges of each panel.

2 Cut two long and two short strips of white paper to fit around the edges of each panel. Draw a line 1 cm (½ in) from the edge. Using a pair of compasses, draw semi-circles along the length of each strip to make a scalloped edge.

3 Cut around the curved edges of each strip, using pinking shears. Punch decorative holes in the centre of each semi-circle and along the straight edges.

➤

4 *Draw a 1 cm (½ in) border around the edges of each panel. Mix the wallpaper paste to a fairly thin consistency and glue the scalloped strips along the drawn lines as shown.*

5 *Trace the flowerpot template and cut from thin card. Fold a sheet of white paper in half and place the straight edge of the template along the fold, holding it in place with bulldog clips. Draw around the template twice for each panel and cut out.*

6 *Carefully position the papercuts on the panels and glue in place with wallpaper paste.*

7 *Draw and then cut out circles of red, yellow and blue paper in different sizes. Fold the red and yellow circles into quarters and cut notches into the curves to make the flowerheads. Glue the red flowers in place, then glue a yellow flower and a blue dot on top.*

8 *Using pinking shears, cut bands of blue paper and glue them to the flowerpots as decoration. Hinge the panels together.*

Silk square **screen**

Open screens are traditionally used as supports for delicate patterned fabrics. This one has panels of silk crêpe de Chine, painted with squares of soft colour. The silk paints make the fabric opaque, so some squares are left unpainted to create a subtle contrast. Each of the panels has a small casing at the top and bottom, allowing them to be attached to the screen from curtain wires rather like net curtains. The faded elegance of the soft colours used in this screen makes it perfect for a bedroom or morning room.

You will need

- Cream silk crêpe de Chine
- Scissors
- Open-panel screen
- Old blanket
- Plastic sheet
- Masking tape
- Chalk pencil and ruler
- Wide paintbrush
- Water-based, iron-fixable silk paints
- Iron
- Curtain wire
- Screw eyes and metal hooks
- Sewing machine
- Matching thread
- Two pairs of cabinet hinges
- Screwdriver

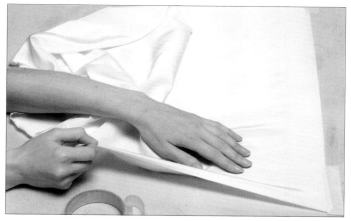

1 Cut a panel of silk to fit each frame, allowing extra for the casings and hems and for the ruched effect. Cover your work surface with the blanket, and tape the plastic over the top. Stretch the silk panels taut and tape them to the work surface, keeping the grain of the fabric straight.

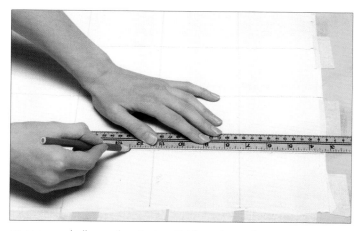

2 Using a chalk pencil and ruler, divide each panel into squares.

3 Place strips of masking tape around the edges of each square to create clean lines. Using a wide brush, fill in the squares with the paints.

4 Leave to dry, then remove the masking tape. Iron the back of the silk, following the paint manufacturer's instructions, to fix the colours.

➤

5 *Trim the silk panels to fit in the frames. Attach lengths of curtain wire to the top and bottom of each frame, using screw eyes and metal hooks.*

6 *Machine hem the edges of each panel, then make a narrow casing at the top and bottom. Hinge the screen together, and slip the panels on to the curtain wire.*

Mosaic firescreen

This mosaic firescreen is an unusual way to hide an open fireplace when it is not in use. The bold pattern has been achieved using only three colours of tesserae (small squares of coloured glass), glued to the front of the firescreen. You can colour the grout with a little acrylic paint to match or contrast with the glass squares. Experiment with different tones of colour for either cool and subdued or hot and vivid effects, but keep the colour range fairly limited. This firescreen is for decorative purposes only and should never be placed near a lighted fire.

You will need

- Squared graph paper
- Pencil
- Pre-cut firescreen
- PVA glue
- Container for mixing
- Glue brush
- Craft knife
- Protective goggles
- Tile nippers
- Mosaic tesserae
- Tile grout
- Acrylic paint (optional)
- Paintbrush (optional)
- Rubber gloves
- Plastic squeegee
- Damp sponge

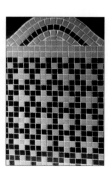

1 *Using the squared paper, draw a design for the firescreen. Prime the surface of the firescreen with a 50/50 mixture of PVA glue and water. Leave to dry, then score with a craft knife to provide a key.*

2 *Wearing protective goggles, use tile nippers to cut the edging tesserae in half.*

3 *Spread a little undiluted PVA glue on the firescreen and start to build up the pattern, using your paper design as a reference. Work on the lefthand side and the top border first. Cover the firescreen feet with tesserae in the same way. Leave to dry overnight.*

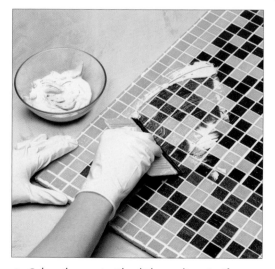

4 *Colour the grout with a little acrylic paint if wished. Wearing rubber gloves, apply tile grout to the tesserae with the squeegee. Work on one section at a time, wiping the surface immediately after each application with a damp sponge. When thoroughly dry, carefully slide the feet into position.*

Architectural screen

During the 18th century it was fashionable to create print rooms, with engravings cut out and attached to walls in formal designs. Here, black-and-white architectural drawings are used in the same way to create a stylish screen, painted an elegant duck-egg blue, a colour very popular in the late 18th century. It would make an elegant addition to a dining room decorated in similar, restrained colours. The bridge motif is applied as a continuous frieze across the panels and is then split with a craft knife when the glue has dried.

You will need

- Pre-cut three-panel screen
- Water-based wood undercoat
- Paintbrush
- Protective face mask
- Fine sandpaper
- Duck-egg-blue emulsion paint
- Black-and-white images
- Cutting mat
- Craft knife
- Pencil and ruler
- PVA glue, diluted 50/50 with water
- Glue brush
- Black acrylic paint
- Clear acrylic varnish
- Varnish brush
- Piano hinges
- Screwdriver

1 Paint the panels with undercoat. Wearing a face mask, lightly rub them down with sandpaper, then apply a coat of duck-egg-blue paint.

2 Place your black-and-white images on a cutting mat and cut around them carefully, using a craft knife.

3 Draw a 4 cm (1½ in) border around the top, bottom and outside edges of the side panels, and at the top and bottom of the central panel. Divide the panels into equal sections and place side by side. Arrange the cut-outs on the panels and glue in position.

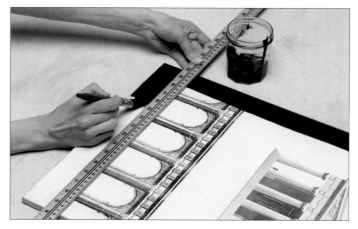

4 Split any continuous designs with a craft knife when the glue has dried. Paint the border with black acrylic paint, using a straight edge as a guide. Leave the panels to dry thoroughly, then seal with two coats of varnish. Hinge the panels together.

Castle
screen

This traditional screen is ingeniously designed so that each panel is a separate element of the fairytale castle. If you intend to use the screen in a child's room, use child-safe paint, varnish and glue, and do not make the angles of the panels too wide when you set up the screen, in order to prevent it from toppling over. For safety's sake, it should not be left with unsupervized children.

You will need

- Two 152 x 60 cm (60 x 24 in) panels of 9 mm (⅜ in) plywood
- 90 x 60 cm (36 x 24 in) panel of 9 mm (⅜ in) plywood
- Pencil and ruler
- Workbench
- Clamps
- Protective face mask
- Coping saw
- Fine sandpaper
- Water-based wood undercoat
- Large and small paintbrushes
- Acrylic paint in a variety of colours
- Tracing paper
- Thin white paper
- Scissors
- Gold acrylic paint
- Artist's paintbrush
- Satin-finish varnish
- Varnish brush
- Drill
- Two pairs of hinges
- Screwdriver

1 *Draw central lines down the two larger plywood panels. Draw diagonal lines from the centre top of each panel to make the arched roof of each tower. Mark a row of crenellations on the top edge of the smaller panel. Clamp each panel in turn firmly to the workbench and, wearing a face mask, cut out all the pieces with a coping saw.*

➤

2 Wearing a face mask, sand all the panels, removing rough edges and rounding off sharp corners. Apply two coats of undercoat to each panel, sanding lightly between coats. Paint all the wall areas and then, using a slightly darker shade, paint in lines of stonework. Stipple parts of the walls with a large brush to give an illusion of depth.

3 Trace the leaf, flower, window and shield templates, and transfer them to the white paper. Draw an arch shape on the paper for the drawbridge. Cut out all the shapes. Place the shield and arch templates on the centre panel and draw around them. Draw the central design on the drawbridge. Paint all the shapes.

4 Place the leaf, flower and window templates on the tower panels and draw around them. Draw tiles on the roofs. Paint in the motifs.

5 Using various shades of blue, paint the roof tiles and leave to dry. Using an artist's paintbrush, outline them with gold paint. Seal the panels with two coats of varnish. Hinge the panels together, drilling pilot holes for the screws first to avoid splitting the wood.

Sunflower screen

The sunflower is an enduring motif in folk and popular art, conveying all that is good and natural. Here, it has been used to bold effect to decorate a small folding screen, which would look wonderful screening a corner of a patio or courtyard. All the flower shapes are cut from plywood and painted with strong, bright colours before being joined to the panels with brass panel pins. In spite of its naïve decoration, this screen is not intended for children and would not be safe as a toy or a play structure.

You will need

- Tracing paper and pencil
- Thin white paper
- Large dinner plate
- Pencil
- Scissors
- Three panels of 9 mm (⅜ in) plywood sheet, each 50 x 122 cm (20 x 48 in)
- Workbench
- Clamps
- Protective face mask
- Coping saw
- Sheet of 4 mm (³⁄₁₆ in) birch plywood
- Fine sandpaper
- Water-based wood undercoat
- Paintbrush
- Acrylic paint, in a variety of colours
- Satin-finish acrylic varnish
- Varnish brush
- Wood glue
- Glue brush
- Brass panel pins
- Tack hammer
- Drill
- Two pairs of hinges
- Screwdriver

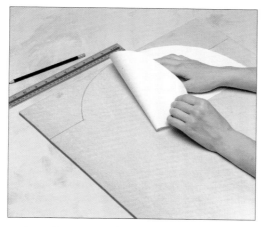

1 Trace the semi-circular template from the back of the book on to white paper (alternatively, draw around a large dinner plate). Cut out the template, place it in the centre top of each panel and draw around it. Draw lines running from either side of the curves to the edge of each panel. Clamp each panel in turn firmly to a workbench, and, wearing a face mask, cut out the top edges with a coping saw.

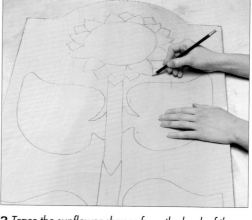

2 Trace the sunflower shapes from the back of the book and transfer them to the birch plywood. For each panel, you need two pairs of leaves, a stalk and a flower. Clamp the plywood firmly to the workbench and, wearing a face mask, cut out all the pieces.

3 Wearing a face mask, thoroughly sand the panels and cut-out shapes to remove any rough edges. Paint all the pieces with two coats of undercoat.

4 Sand the panels lightly, then apply a coat of blue acrylic paint. Darken the blue paint by adding dark green and make crescent-shaped brushstrokes at regular intervals across the panels.

➤

5 Paint the sunflowers, leaves and stalks. Seal the surface of all the shapes and the panels with two coats of varnish. Leave to dry.

6 Glue the shapes to the panels and hold in place with brass panel pins. Hinge the panels together, drilling small pilot holes for the screws first to avoid splitting the wood.

Floral chimney board

Chimney boards first became popular in the 18th century. Initially, designs were painted on to board and cut out, but découpage soon followed. The extensive range of subject matter included soldiers, tradesmen, servants, farm and domestic animals, plants and flowers. Like firescreens, chimney boards brighten up empty fireplaces during the summer months, blocking draughts as well. They should never be placed near a lighted fire.

You will need

- Tracing paper
- Pencil
- Large sheet of white paper
- Floral giftwrap
- Scissors
- Re-usable adhesive gum
- 8 mm (¼ in) and 16 mm (½ in) medium-density fibreboard (MDF)
- Workbench
- Clamps
- Protective face mask
- Coping saw
- Fine sandpaper
- PVA glue
- Container for mixing
- Glue brush
- Emulsion paint: white and dark green
- Paintbrush
- Blue acrylic paint
- Artist's paintbrush
- Clear acrylic varnish
- Varnish brush
- Bradawl
- Pair of hinges
- Screwdriver

1 Draw a simple vase shape and transfer it to a large sheet of white paper. Cut out a selection of flowers from giftwrap and arrange them above the vase. When you are satisfied with the design, stick the flowers in place with small pieces of re-usable adhesive gum. Fill any gaps with small flowers.

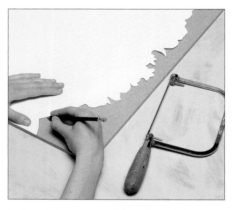

2 Carefully cut around the edges of the design. Place the cut-out face down on the 8 mm (¼ in) MDF and draw around it, leaving a small border around the edge as the paper may expand slightly when glued in position. Draw and transfer a foot support on to the thicker MDF and clamp to the workbench. Wearing a face mask, cut out the shapes, using a coping saw. Sand the edges smooth.

3 Seal the cut-outs with a coat of diluted PVA glue. Using the artist's paintbrush, paint the vase white, then add fine blue lines in acrylic paint. Paint the rest of the front of the board and the foot dark green and leave to dry.

4 Transfer the flowers from the paper to the board one by one in the same order, and glue in position. When dry, apply three coats of clear acrylic varnish to the front and back of the board and the foot.

5 Place the foot in position on the back of the board, 1 cm (½ in) up from the bottom edge. Mark the screw holes on the board and foot with a bradawl, then attach the hinges to join them together.

Off the Wall

F RIVOLOUS AND FUN ARE THE WORDS TO DESCRIBE THESE SCREENS. VIVID COLOURS, BOLD MOTIFS, ABSTRACT OPTICAL EFFECTS AND UNUSUAL MATERIALS MAKE THEM A FORCE TO BE RECKONED WITH. THESE ARE NOT SCREENS FOR THE SHY AND RETIRING, NOR FOR THE PURIST, BUT THEY WILL APPEAL TO THOSE WHO LOVE IMAGINATIVE DECORATING SOLUTIONS. SEVERAL OF THE SCREENS USE FOUND OBJECTS, INCLUDING PLASTIC BOTTLES AND ALUMINIUM DRINKS CANS. LEARN TO DEVELOP A MAGPIE'S ENTHUSIASM FOR THE SHINY, THE COLOURFUL AND THE DOWNRIGHT IRRESISTIBLE, AND PRESERVE YOUR DISCOVERIES BY INTEGRATING THEM INTO A UNIQUE, PERSONAL SCREEN.

Gallery

An eclectic range of materials has been used to create these exciting and undeniably eccentric screens. From telephone wire to pasta shells, the everyday minutiae of modern life are exploited to provide a new "take" on the familiar. Almost anything can be incorporated into a screen – even discarded items develop a new beauty when they are suspended in a length of sheer mesh or used in a stunning mosaic triptych, for example.

As well as recycled materials, other decorative products such as paint, sculpted paper and, the ultimate in kitsch, fake fur all appear here, to inspire the senses and start the creative juices flowing.

Left: *This highly decorative screen has brightly coloured wooden supports that frame a riot of fantastic shapes divided into different-sized compartments. These were folded, quilled and spiralled from heavy watercolour paper that had been hand-painted with reactive dyes.*
Paul Johnson

Below: *The wild and wacky Dalmatian spotted fabric gives this screen excitement and glamour. Each screen panel has a "window" made from expanded steel mesh, which accentuates the screen's enigmatic, slightly dangerous appearance. The mesh is framed with lengths of black cord to hide the fixings.*

Tessa Brown

Above: *This screen owes its intricate netted appearance to the lengths of telephone wire that run up and down the panels. A variety of plastics, including polypropylene strapping tape, strips of plastic sheeting and plastic packing tape, have been woven through the telephone wire to make a dynamic contrast. The uprights and curved edges of the screen are wooden.*

Lois Walpole

Left: *This exuberantly coloured folding screen is covered with flowers and elemental symbols, creating a riot of summer colour. The panels have been submerged in layers of motifs torn directly from sheets of hand-coloured recycled paper, embellished with pastel and ink for extra texture.*

Amanda Pearce

Left: *Bright colours and a bold design make this screen exuberant and fun. The classical imagery of centaur and faun is updated to an irreverent cartoon-like quality. The screen panels are made from thin hardboard framed with lengths of pine. Each panel was covered with layers of papier mâché and decorated with acrylic paint.*

Marion Elliot

Above left: *One of the most familiar of all screen styles is the hospital screen, used to give some privacy in a bustling ward. The design has not changed much in the years since it was first introduced. This is a typical four-panel folding screen on a tubular metal frame set on castor wheels. Each panel is covered with flame-retardant fabric.*

Hospital Metalcraft Ltd

Above right: *The themes of this elegantly eccentric room divider are dining and gardening, hence the inclusion of pasta, beans, seeds and sweet wrappers. The base fabric is nylon micro-filament, which was made up into a mesh on a knitting machine. Tiny pockets were then knitted into the fabric, filled with a variety of small objects, and sealed.*

Susie Freeman

Aluminium butterfly
firescreen

These beautiful, shimmering butterflies are made from recycled aluminium drinks cans, which are soft and easy to cut with ordinary scissors. The cans' colourful printed labelling forms an integral part of the design, especially when sanded to give a patchy, iridescent effect. The metal is easily embossed by drawing on the back with a ballpoint pen. This firescreen is for decoration only, to hide an empty fireplace in the summer. Never place it near a lighted fire.

You will need

- Pre-cut firescreen
- Water-based wood primer
- Paintbrush
- Terracotta satin-finish wood paint
- Protective gloves
- Empty aluminium drinks cans
- Scissors
- Pencil
- Thin white card
- Thick scrap card
- Ballpoint pen
- Fine sandpaper
- Pinking shears
- Dressmaker's wheel
- Bradawl
- Brass escutcheon pins
- Tack hammer

1 *Paint the surfaces of the firescreen and the feet with wood primer. When dry, apply two coats of terracotta paint.*

2 *Wearing protective gloves, cut pieces from the drinks cans and gently flatten the metal. Trace the butterfly shapes from the back of the book on to white card and cut out. Hold each template against a piece of aluminium and carefully cut around it.*

3 *Place the butterfly cut-outs face down on the thick scrap card. Emboss designs into the metal by drawing on it with a ballpoint pen. Lightly sand the fronts of the butterflies to distress the bright and shiny surface of the metal.*

4 *Using pinking shears, cut thin strips of aluminium to fit around the edges of the screen. Run a dressmaker's wheel along the reverse of each strip to make a decorative line of raised dots. Using a bradawl, make holes in the strips and the edges of the butterflies. Attach them to the firescreen, using escutcheon pins and a tack hammer.*

Woven cardboard
screen

Heavy corrugated cardboard can be woven into very sturdy panels to make an excellent screen. The cardboard is light enough for the screen to be moved easily from room to room, or even outside as an impromptu windbreak if the weather is dry. The cardboard is painted with dazzling vertical stripes which, when woven, look like traditional wattle panels, updated for the late 20th century. The two panels are edged with wooden strips to make them rigid, and lashed together with cord.

You will need

- Corrugated-cardboard boxes of single-wall construction
- Scissors
- Paint tray
- Water-based paint: white and assorted colours
- Small paint roller
- Stapler
- Bradawl
- Strong, coloured nylon cord
- Large darning needle
- Wooden batten
- Small saw
- Drill
- Small sponge
- Large clips
- Wood offcut

1 *Cut panels of cardboard from the boxes, making sure that they are as flat and smooth as possible. Paint one side of each panel white, then add a pattern of multi-coloured stripes with the paint roller. Paint the other side in the same way, so that the finished screen is reversible.*

2 *Cut the cardboard into 10 cm (4 in) wide strips, cutting across the corrugations. Place six strips side by side, folding under 2 cm (¾ in) at the ends of each strip. Weave through a horizontal strip and staple the ends of the vertical strips to it.*

➤

3 Continue to weave in horizontal strips until you reach the desired height. Turn under the sides of the horizontals and staple to the verticals as you work.

4 Using a bradawl, pierce holes in the top and bottom edges of each screen panel. Sew a line of decorative stitching through the holes, using the nylon cord and darning needle.

5 Cut four lengths of batten the same length as the sides of the screen panels. Drill a hole every 4 cm (1½ in) along the length of the battens. Sponge each piece with paint. Clip the battens to the edges of the screen panels. Place the edge of each panel on an offcut of wood and pierce through the drilled holes to the cardboard, using a bradawl.

6 Sew the battens to the edges of the panels with nylon cord.

7 Place the panels together, matching the edges carefully. Lash them with cord, passing the needle underneath the top strip of batten, over the join to the back, and under the second strip.

Translucent paper
screen

Here, an old Japanese-style three-panel screen has been transformed into a new and exciting focal point for a modern room – the perfect complement to bright plastics, shiny metal surfaces and industrial accessories. The tissue-paper panels glow with transparent pools of colour. This effect is achieved with very simple materials – scraps of coloured acetate, offcuts of bubblewrap and small pieces of interesting paper.

You will need

- Japanese-style three-panel screen with tissue-paper squares
- Screwdriver
- Acrylic paint, in three bright colours
- Paintbrush
- Scraps of paper, bubblewrap and coloured acetate
- Strong glue
- Adhesive tape
- Craft knife
- Protective goggles
- Staple gun
- Clear acrylic varnish and brush
- Enamel paint, in three colours to match the acrylic paint
- Artist's paintbrush

1 *Remove the hinges from the screen to divide it into separate panels. Paint the wooden frames different bright colours.*

2 *Assemble the scraps of paper, bubblewrap and acetate into individual squares. Secure with glue and tape.*

3 *Using a craft knife, remove whole and partial sections from the tissue-paper squares. Leave some tissue-paper squares complete.*

4 *Working on the back of each panel, attach the coloured squares to the screen with glue, tape and staples. Wear protective goggles.*

➤

5 *Apply a coat of acrylic varnish to the wooden frames. Also varnish the plain tissue-paper squares to make them translucent.*

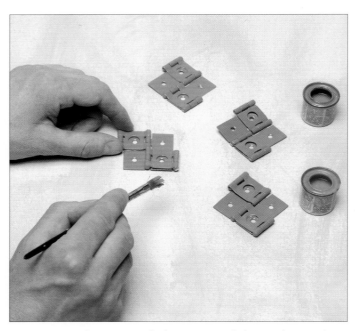

6 *Using enamel paint, paint the hinges to match the wooden panels. Leave to dry, then reassemble the screen.*

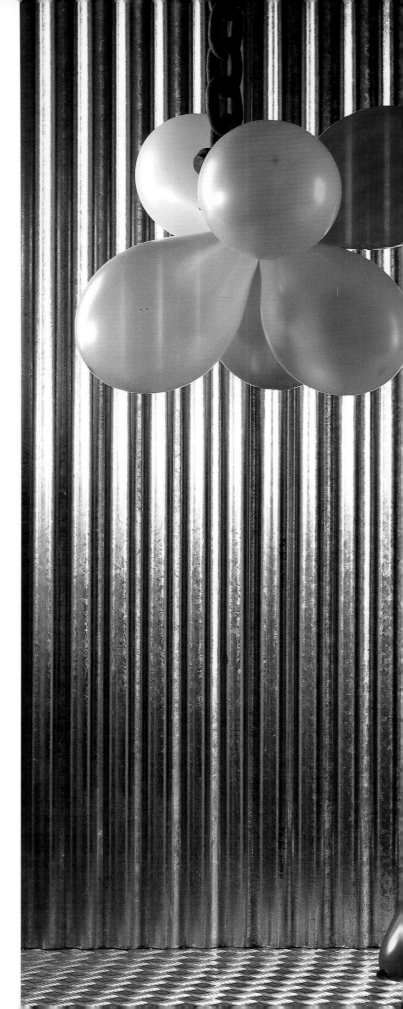

Pocket **screen**

Intended for a child's bedroom, this screen is both functional and fun. It can be adapted to cover a doorway, screen off a play area or to hang around a bunk bed to create a secret den. The pockets are useful for storing toys and shoes, or cotton wool, wipes and clothes in a baby's nursery. The beauty of this screen is its versatility, and the fact that it can be made quickly and cheaply using a mixture of fabrics left over from previous sewing projects. The screen can be suspended from a pole using curtain hooks, coloured tapes or cord.

You will need

- Tracing paper and pencil
- Thin white paper
- Scissors
- Plain and patterned cotton fabrics
- Dressmaker's pins
- Sewing machine
- Matching thread
- Iron
- Sewing needle
- Braids, fringing and pompons
- Embroidery thread
- Cotton lining fabric
- Eyelet punch
- 1 cm (½ in) metal eyelets
- Tack hammer

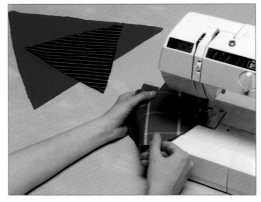

1 *Draw simple pocket shapes, transfer them to paper and cut out. Cut two large and two small fabric pieces for each pocket. Right sides facing, pin and machine stitch the two halves of each pocket together around three sides. Clip the corners and turn right side out. Press and slip stitch the openings.*

2 *Decorate both sections of each pocket with braids, fringing and pompons. Join the two sections of each pocket with embroidery thread, using a long running stitch.*

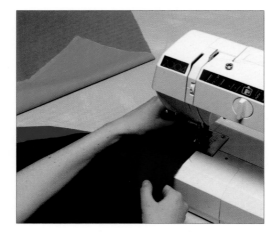

3 *Cut squares of brightly coloured fabric measuring 51 x 51 cm (20 x 20 in) to make the screen. Right sides facing, pin and stitch the squares together. Stitch a pocket to each square.*

4 *For the lining, cut a piece of cotton fabric the same size as the screen. Right sides facing, pin and stitch the lining to the screen, leaving a 1 cm (½ in) seam allowance and the bottom edge open. Turn right side out. Press the raw edges to the inside and slip stitch or machine stitch the opening. Using an eyelet punch, make evenly spaced holes along the top of the screen and attach metal eyelets.*

Woven window screen

Here, humble plastic drinks bottles are ingeniously recycled to make a screen designed to cover the lower half of a sash window. The screen is suspended from hooks on either side of the window frame, and so can easily be removed to let in more daylight, or be placed in another location. A subtle touch of colour is added with strips of plastic cut from green bottles – use several colours, if you wish, for a more dramatic effect. Dark colours, however, will block out more light rather than subtly diffusing it.

You will need

- Clear and green plastic drinks bottles
- Scissors
- Hole punch
- Thin wooden batten
- Small saw
- Thin wire and drill, or wood glue and panel pins
- Protective goggles
- Staple gun

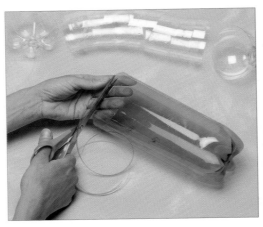

1   Remove the tops and bottoms from all the bottles. Starting at the bottom of each bottle, cut continuous spiral strips from the plastic. The clear strips should be about 3 cm (1¼ in) wide and the green strips thin enough to thread through a hole made by your hole punch. Cut enough strips to cover your window frame.

2   Using the hole punch, make two holes along the top and bottom edges of the clear strips. Thread the green strips through the holes.

3   Cut four strips of batten to fit the window frame. Join the corners of the wood by drilling holes and threading them with thin wire, or use wood glue and panel pins. Wearing goggles, use a staple gun to attach the clear strips at 8 cm (3 in) intervals at the top and bottom of the screen.

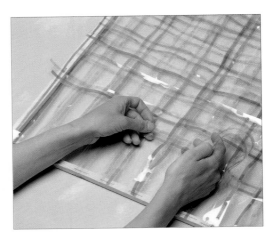

4   When all the vertical strips are in position, weave the horizontals in and out. First secure one end of each strip to the side of the screen with a staple, then staple the other end when you have woven it through. Trim the excess plastic around the screen.

Flower-power
room divider

This cheerful fabric room divider is perfect for a child's bedroom, creating a den in a quiet corner, separating homework and play areas, or defining the space between two beds – and two children! The felt daisies can be removed and rearranged, or changed for a different motif made in the same way as described below. The tabs at the top are fastened with press studs, so the divider can be removed easily from the curtain pole for laundering.

You will need

- Pencil
- Thin, white paper
- Scissors
- Felt, in assorted bright colours
- Dressmaker's pins
- Embroidery thread, in assorted bright colours
- Embroidery and sewing needles
- Velcro
- Sewing machine (optional)
- Wadding
- Heavyweight cotton fabrics, in assorted bright colours and dark blue
- 3 cm (1¼ in) self-covering buttons
- Fabric glue
- Large press studs

1 *Make large flower and flower centre templates, and cut out. Pin the templates on to the felt and cut as many flowers as required. Using contrasting embroidery thread, sew French knots on the flower centres.*

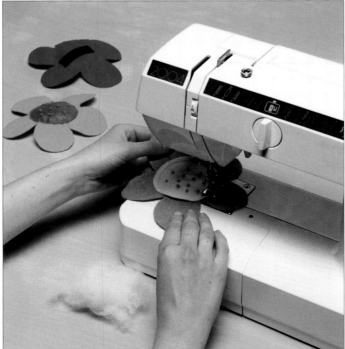

2 *Cut a 3.5 cm (1½ in) strip of Velcro for each flower and sew the hooked side to the back. Handsew or machine stitch the flower centres to the flowers, leaving a 2 cm (¾ in) gap in the stitching. Lightly stuff the centres with wadding, then slip stitch the gap closed.*

➤

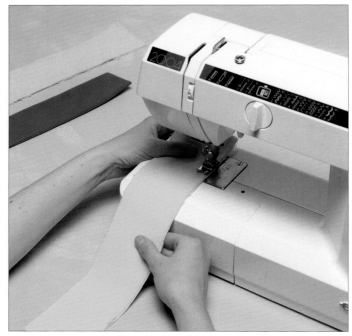

3 To make the tabs, cut strips of brightly coloured fabrics 33 x 7.5 cm (13 x 3 in). Right sides facing, stitch the strips together in pairs around three sides. Clip the corners and turn right side out.

4 Make small flower and flower centre templates. Cut one flower and centre for each tab from the felt. Snip a hole in the centre of each flower. Place the button fronts on the flower centres, sew a line of running stitch around the edge and pull to gather. Push the button shanks through the flowers and snap on the backs. Glue small dots of contrasting felt to the flower centres. Sew a flower to the end of each tab.

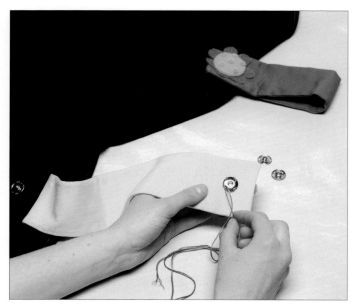

5 Cut the dark blue fabric to the desired dimensions for the divider. Cut a strip of fabric the same width and 20 cm (8 in) deep to make a facing. Pin the tabs at regular intervals along the front top edge of the divider. Place the facing over the tabs and pin it to the divider, right sides facing. Stitch, clip the corners and turn the facing to the back.

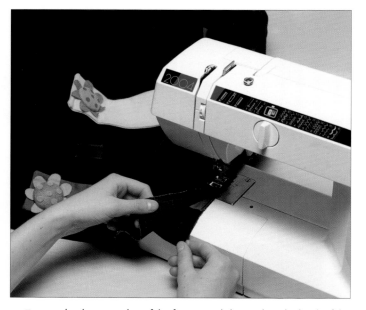

6 Turn under the raw edge of the facing and slip stitch to the back of the divider. Glue and stitch the remaining halves of the Velcro strips on the front. Hem the side seams. Sew large press studs to the backs of the tabs and to the front of the divider. Hang the room divider, then hem the bottom edge.

Bright bird screen

Some screens are discreet and hardly noticed, while others make their presence felt. This screen is as important as any other item of furniture, creating a strong focal point in a room. The bold, simple motifs are inspired by a Mexican carpet, and the panels are cut from a sheet of medium-density fibreboard (MDF), which is easy to manipulate and decorate. It is, however, essential to wear a protective face mask when cutting this material, as a very fine dust is produced. The finished screen has a shaped cut-out at the top of the panels. These are quite tricky to cut, so leave the tops plain, if wished.

You will need

- Tracing paper and pencil
- Paper
- Scissors
- Three 150 x 45 cm (59 x 18 in)
- panels of medium-density fibreboard (MDF)
- Workbench
- Clamps
- Protective face mask
- Coping saw
- Fine sandpaper
- Water-based wood primer
- Large and small paintbrushes
- Craft knife
- Cutting mat
- Ruler
- Acrylic paint, in assorted colours
- Matt acrylic varnish
- Varnish brush
- Four cabinet hinges
- Screwdriver

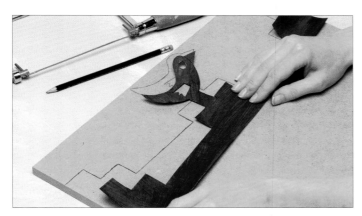

1 Draw a paper template for the top of the panels and cut out. Draw around the template on to each sheet of MDF. Clamp each panel firmly to a workbench and, wearing a protective face mask, cut out the design with a coping saw. Sand the edges smooth.

2 Paint both sides and the edges of each panel with primer. Apply two or three coats to achieve a smooth surface. Wearing the face mask, lightly sand the panels between each coat.

3 Trace the templates from the back of the book and transfer to paper. Cut out with a craft knife, using a cutting mat. It may help you to determine the arrangement of your design on the undercoated panels if you cut the templates from coloured paper.

4 Rearrange the templates on the panels until you are satisfied with the design, then draw around them. Draw a 1 cm (½ in) border around the edge of each panel.

5 *Using acrylic paints in your chosen colours, start to fill in the designs and the borders.*

6 *Fill in the background colour. When the fronts of the panels are dry, paint the backs and then leave the panels to dry overnight. Seal the panels with three coats of matt acrylic varnish. Leave the varnish to dry, then hinge together.*

Plastic pocket
screen

Clear-plastic document holders (readily available from stationers) are ingeniously used to create this multi-functional space-age screen. It makes a witty display case for a collection of objects such as small toys, or perhaps printed ephemera – an updated version of the wooden printer's type tray. The beauty of this screen is that it can be rearranged and added to indefinitely, or adapted to different locations in the home, while at the same time keeping cherished possessions safe and free from dust.

You will need

- Clear-plastic document holders
- Scissors
- Wood offcut
- Hammer and punch
- Metal eyelets
- Eyelet punch
- Small objects such as toys, games and pictures
- Jointed split-metal rings
- Pliers
- Metal pole and pair of pole supports

1 Cut down the document holders to make square pockets. Place each pocket on an offcut of wood and make a pair of holes top and bottom, using a hammer and punch.

2 Reinforce the bottom pair of holes with metal eyelets. Fill each pocket with small objects.

3 Attach metal eyelets to the top pair of holes. Join the pockets together vertically, using split-metal rings and pliers, to make long strips.

4 Thread the strips on to a metal pole. Fix the pole supports where desired and add the pole, making sure that it is firmly in position.

Practicalities

WHETHER YOU WISH TO REVAMP AN EXISTING SCREEN, TO TRANSFORM A SECONDHAND BARGAIN OR TO MAKE A SCREEN FROM SCRATCH, IT IS POSSIBLE TO DO SO WITHOUT A GREAT DEAL OF OUTLAY. YOU DO NOT NEED TO BE A WOODWORK EXPERT EITHER – PRE-CUT SCREEN BLANKS ARE AVAILABLE IN A WIDE RANGE OF SIZES.

IF YOU ARE UNSURE OF YOUR ARTISTIC SKILLS, THERE ARE STENCILS, STAMPS AND PAINT EFFECTS GALORE THAT WILL ENABLE YOU TO CREATE A SCREEN THAT YOU CAN SHOW OFF WITH PRIDE.

General techniques

There are several different types of traditional screen. Pre-cut blanks in a variety of classic shapes such as Gothic, serpentine, straight-topped and curved can be purchased by mail order from specialist suppliers. Alternatively, you can cut screen panels to your own design from MDF (medium-density fibreboard) or plywood panels. Whichever approach you choose, the following general techniques will ensure a professional finish. Always wear a protective face mask when sawing wood or MDF, as a very fine dust is produced.

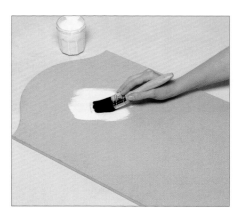

1 *If you wish to paint your screen, the surface will need to be prepared first to provide a good "ground" for the paint. Unsealed wood should be sealed with a primer. If possible, use a water-based wood primer as this dries quickly and is much more pleasant to work with than the oil-based version. Always take care to work in well-ventilated conditions when using primers.*

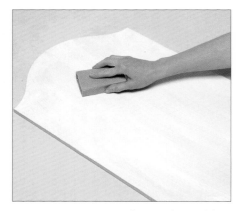

2 *Wearing a protective face mask, sand the panels lightly. Apply two coats of undercoat. If you are using water-based paints, you can use a water-based undercoat. If you use oil-based paints, you will need to prepare the panels with an oil-based undercoat. All oil-based paints give off unpleasant fumes and should only be used in well-ventilated areas. Sand the panels lightly between coats.*

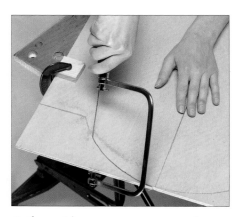

3 *If you wish to cut your own screen, sheets of MDF and plywood 9–10 mm (⅜ in) thick are ideal. They often come in standard sizes such as 240 x 120 cm (8 x 4 ft) that are difficult to handle, so ask your wood merchant to cut them to size first. Draw the design at the top of the panels freehand, or use a template. Firmly clamp the panel to a workbench and cut out the shape, using a coping saw.*

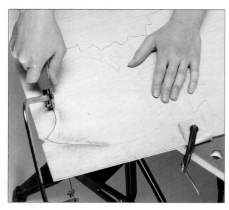

4 *When cutting more intricate shapes, clamp the sheet to the workbench and keep adjusting the blade of the saw to enable you to get into awkward corners or to cut curves.*

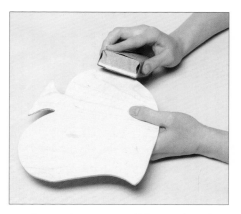

5 *After you have cut out all the panels and smaller pieces, remove any rough edges and sharp corners by sanding. Again, always wear a protective face mask.*

6 *Open-panel screens are often used to display lengths of decorative fabric. The fabric can simply be stapled or glued to the panels, but it looks much nicer if it is suspended from lengths of curtain wire. Attach this to the wood, using screw eyes and metal hooks.*

7 *If you are covering a screen with fabric, there is no need to prepare the surface of the panels. Although not strictly necessary, a layer of wadding placed beneath the fabric covering does give a luxurious, slightly upholstered appearance. Choose a mediumweight wadding and cut a piece for the front and back, or the front only, of each panel. Spread a layer of PVA glue over the panels and press the wadding in place. Leave the panels to dry for 1–2 hours before covering them with fabric.*

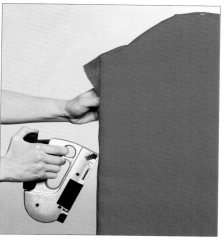

8 *Cut a length of fabric about 5 cm (2 in) larger all round than each panel. Working with the panel upright, drape a length of fabric over it, making sure that the grain of the fabric is straight. Staple the fabric to the middle of the top edge, then at the bottom, then either side, pulling it taut at each edge. Once the fabric is pinned at all four points, start to staple it in position around the screen, pulling it taut and working from side to side towards the corners. Wear protective goggles when using a staple gun.*

9 *Once the panel is covered and you are happy with the fit of the fabric on the frame, carefully trim back the excess fabric to about 3 mm (⅛ in) from the staples.*

10 *Cover the backs of the panels in the same way, but this time turn under the raw edges of each piece of fabric before stapling it over the raw edges of the front piece.*

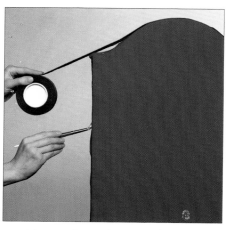

11 *Measure the top, bottom and side edges of one side panel. Cut two pieces of narrow petersham ribbon to this length, plus 6 cm (2¼ in). Measure the top and bottom edges of the central panel and cut a length of ribbon to fit, plus 3 cm (1¼ in). Apply PVA glue around the edges of the panels and press the ribbon into place, turning under the raw ends.*

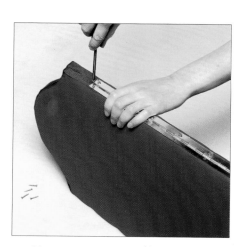

12 *You can use a variety of hinges to join screen panels together, but long brass piano hinges are the most stable and stylish. If your screen has more than two panels, attach the hinges so that they open in opposite directions, zigzag fashion.*

Making an open-panel
screen

A simple open-panel screen is easy to construct from a softwood such as pine. The panels can be painted, colour-washed, or simply sealed with varnish. Fill each panel with a variety of different materials, including plain or patterned fabric, paper, sheet metal, peg board, Perspex, beads, coloured cord, raffia – the choice is yours. Always wear a protective face mask when cutting and sanding wood or MDF (medium-density fibreboard).

1 *Measure two uprights and two crossbars for each panel. The open-panel screens in this book have uprights measuring 150 cm (60 in) and crossbars measuring 48 cm (19 in), and are cut from lengths of 5 x 2.5 cm (2 x 1 in) pine. Wearing a protective face mask, clamp the wood and cut to length.*

2 *The panels are joined with half-lap joints. Measure a 5 x 5 x 2.5 cm (2 x 2 x 1 in) square at either end of the crossbars and the top of each upright, using a set square and pencil. Measure a second square 20 cm (8 in) from the lower ends of each upright.*

3 *Clamp each length of wood firmly and then, using a tenon saw, cut down the side of each square to the centre line. Cut down both sides of the squares at the lower ends of the uprights.*

4 *Firmly clamp each pine length vertically and carefully saw down to meet the first cut, making a square recess. Firmly clamp the lower uprights. Wearing protective goggles, carefully chisel out the remaining sides of the squares to make recesses as before.*

5 *Sand the joints thoroughly to remove any rough edges and ensure a snug fit.*

6 *Mark the centre of each joint. Clamp the pine lengths and drill a hole at each point. Spread wood glue on each joint and fit the panels together, making sure that each joint is a right angle. Screw the joints together.*

7 If a natural look is desired, simply seal the panels with two coats of matt acrylic varnish and leave to dry thoroughly.

8 To create a colour-washed effect – changing the colour of the wood while allowing the grain to show through – apply diluted emulsion paint liberally to the wood. Wait about 15 minutes, then wipe away the excess paint with a soft cloth to reveal the grain. Protect the paintwork with a coat of matt acrylic varnish.

9 Several types of hinge are suitable for joining the panels together. One of the most practical is the butterfly hinge, which sits flush to the wood, allowing the screen to be folded completely flat. Attach one side of the hinge to the edge of a panel, with the hinge resting along the edge of the wood.

10 Place the second panel on top of the first panel and then screw the centre of the hinge into position.

11 Ordinary hinges can also be used to join the panels, but they need to be sited in a small recess first. To make the recess, draw around one half of the hinge on the side of each panel. Clamp each panel firmly to a workbench and, wearing protective goggles, carefully chisel away the wood to the depth of the hinge. Screw the hinges in place.

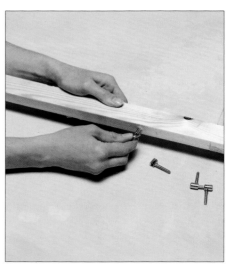

12 If you would like to be able to separate the screen panels, an alternative to fixed hinges is a two-part coupling device. Screw this into the sides of the panels, and simply unhook it when desired.

Materials

*A*ll the basic materials required to make or decorate screens can be purchased from craft and hobby shops, art suppliers, hardware stores or timber merchants. Screen blanks are available by mail order from specialist suppliers. Wherever possible, use water-based sealers, primers, undercoats, paints and varnishes, as they are much more pleasant to handle and work with than the oil-based versions.

MDF (medium-density fibreboard) comes in large sheets in several widths. It is easy to cut and will not warp unless it becomes wet. It has an extremely smooth surface that can be painted, découpaged, stencilled, gilded, colour-washed and distressed. Always wear a protective face mask when cutting or sanding MDF, as a very fine dust is produced.

Plywood also comes in a variety of sizes and widths. It is perfect for making decorative cut-outs (which are simplest to cut with a coping saw), as well as screen panels. Wear a protective face mask when sawing or sanding plywood.

Softwoods such as pine are used for making open-panel screens. Lengths of 5 x 2.5 cm (2 x 1 in) planed wood are good for screens, being lightweight and manageable. Wear a protective face mask when cutting or sanding softwoods.

Thin wooden dowel is a decorative yet practical device for joining the uprights of softwood screen panels together. It is also a useful alternative to curtain wire for suspending fabric or paper panels from open-frame screens.

Wadding is a soft, thick padding fabric made from polyester or cotton. It comes in several different weights and widths. Mediumweight wadding can be glued to screen panels before they are covered with fabric.

Fabrics of many kinds, from hessian to silk, can be used to cover screens. Avoid very shiny, slippery fabrics, or those that stretch. Use furnishing fabrics where possible, as light dress weights are less hardwearing. Washable fabrics that can be sponged clean are the most practical. Avoid fabrics with very large motifs and repeats, as they may look out of proportion to the screen panels.

Thin petersham ribbon can be found in haberdashery departments. It has a distinctive ribbed surface and is very strong. It is used to neaten the raw edges around fabric-covered screen panels.

Wood undercoat is applied to screen panels if they are to be painted, to prepare the surface. A coat of primer may be applied first. If you are using water-based paints to decorate your screen, use a water-based undercoat. Oil-based paints require an oil-based undercoat. Always ensure that you have good ventilation when using undercoat.

Acrylic paints are water-based, but quickly dry to a hard, plastic, waterproof finish. They cover well and produce an intense depth of colour. Some colours contain toxic pigments, so always follow the manufacturer's safety instructions.

Enamel spray paint can be used to apply a fine coat of paint to a wide range of materials, including Perspex, some

metals and wood. It should only be used in a very well-ventilated area, and protective gloves and a face mask should always be worn.

Iron-fixable fabric paints are thick, and suitable for use with natural fabrics. They come in a wide range of colours and can be intermixed within the same brand. Always choose a non-toxic variety, and follow the manufacturer's safety instructions closely.

Water-based silk paints are thin and brilliantly coloured, and flow quickly over the surface of the fabric. They are often used in conjunction with water-based guttas and outliners, which clog the mesh of the silk, making a barrier that the paint cannot flow past. Choose non-toxic paints and guttas, and follow the manufacturer's safety instructions.

Varnish may be water- or oil-based, and comes in various finishes from matt to high gloss. Use water-based varnish in conjunction with water-based paints, and the oil-based variety with oil-based paints. Always ensure that you have good ventilation when using varnish.

Fine-grade sandpaper is used to smooth wood between applications of undercoat or paint, to finish edges, to remove sharp corners after sawing, and to prepare joints before gluing. Always wear a protective face mask when sanding.

PVA glue is a strong, white glue that dries to a clear finish. It can be diluted to découpage cut-outs on to screen panels and can also be used as a varnish, although it is not waterproof.

Spray adhesive is good for positioning

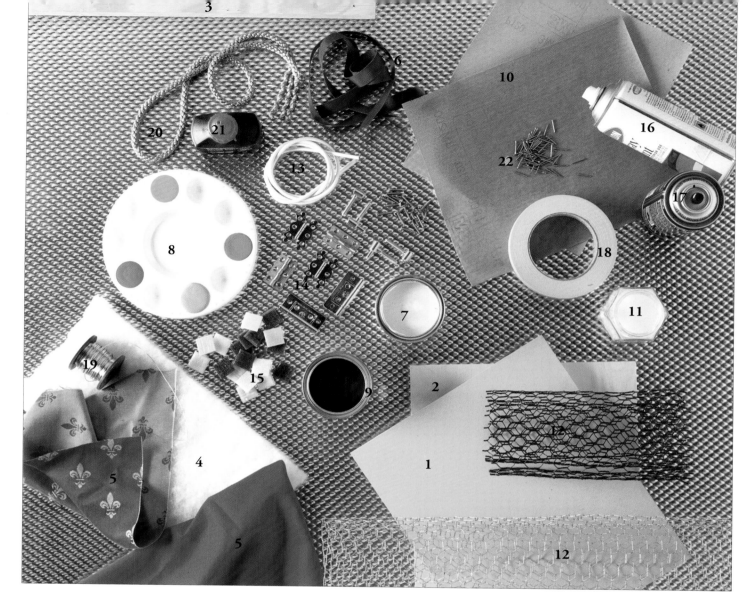

motifs temporarily on a screen panel before they are finally glued in position. Only use in a well-ventilated area, and always wear a protective face mask.

Chicken wire is made from galvanized steel wire and comes in several widths and hole sizes. Wearing protective gloves, the wire is easily manipulated, and can be cut with wire-cutters or the cutting edge on a pair of pliers.

Fine wire is useful for keeping items in position when you are using chicken wire or florist's materials. It can be cut with wire-cutters or the cutting edge on a pair of pliers.

Stencil film is made from clear acetate and can be cut into any design. Tape it to

a cutting mat, or hold it securely, and cut out using a craft knife. Acetate is easier to use than stencilling card as you can see through it and position it in exactly the right place.

Curtain wire is covered in plastic and can be bought from haberdashery departments. Attach it to the top and bottom corners of open-panel screens using screw eyes and metal hooks to suspend panels of fabric and paper.

Hinges come in a variety of styles. Use flush-fitting butterfly hinges or long piano hinges if possible, so that the screen panels will close completely flat.

Mosaic tesserae are small squares of glass. They come in many different

Above: *1 MDF; 2 plywood; 3 softwood; 4 wadding; 5 fabric; 6 petersham ribbon; 7 wood undercoat; 8 acrylic paints; 9 varnish 10 sandpaper; 11 PVA glue; 12 chicken wire; 13 curtain wire; 14 hinges; 15 mosaic tesserae; 16 enamel spray paint; 17 spray adhesive; 18 masking tape; 19 fine wire; 20 decorative cord; 21 wood glue; 22 panel pins*

colours, including gold. They can be used intact or cut to any shape using special metal nippers or tile cutters.

Masking tape is paper tape that is repositionable once it is stuck down. It is useful for stretching lengths of fabric before they are painted.

Equipment

Most of the equipment required to make or cover screens is readily available, and much of it you may already have. Specialist items such as silk-painting frames can be purchased from craft and hobby shops, or by mail order. When using any sort of tool, it is a wise precaution to wear protective goggles and/or a respiratory or dust face mask – in some instances it is essential. A very useful piece of equipment is a portable workbench as this makes clamping, sawing, applying hinges and chiselling much easier; otherwise, use a fixed workbench and bench vice.

A coping saw is good for cutting decorative edges into screen panels, and for cutting small, intricate shapes. The blade is moveable and can be adjusted to allow access to awkward corners.

A staple gun is used to attach fabric or other materials – such as cardboard – to screen panels. Staple guns are available in different strengths, so do not pick one that is so powerful that it splits the wood! Wear protective goggles when you are using a staple gun.

Crosshead screws are used to attach hinges to screen panels. The screws should have long enough shanks to keep the hinges firmly in position.

Brass-headed escutcheon pins are short, decorative nails used to keep small cut-outs in position on screen panels.

Upholsterer's tacks are dome-headed pins, used to keep fabric in place. They are available in different finishes, including chrome and brass.

Paintbrushes come in many guises. For applying primer and undercoat to an average-sized screen panel, a 5 cm (2 in) decorator's brush is appropriate. Buy the best quality that you can afford, as cheap brushes tend to shed hairs. For finer work such as filling in designs, use an artist's sable or nylon brush. Clean brushes immediately after use, following the paint manufacturer's instructions.

A crosshead screwdriver is used with crosshead screws. A ratchet or electric screwdriver makes tasks such as applying long piano hinges easier on the hands.

A pencil and ruler are essential for dividing a screen panel accurately if you are applying a measured design.

A craft knife is very useful for accurate cutting. Always work on a cutting mat, and cut away from your body, turning the work as necessary.

A lightweight tack hammer is good for hammering in short nails such as panel pins. A ballhead hammer is good for general use.

A protective face mask should always be worn when sawing, sanding or working with materials such as solvents, spray paints, and glues and paints that give off strong fumes.

Rubber gloves should be worn to protect the hands when using materials such as spray paint or tile grout. If your skin is sensitive and easily irritated, it is wise to wear gloves even when handling PVA glue and solvent-based products, water- and oil-based paints and varnishes, and always with any cleaning agents such as white spirit.

Heavy-duty protective gloves should always be worn when handling materials such as wire and chicken wire, to protect the skin from scratches.

A sewing machine is used to make some of the screens and room dividers in this book. A basic machine that works straight and zigzag stitches makes large-scale projects much simpler and quicker to complete.

Steel dressmaker's pins should be used if possible as they will not mark fabric. Always remove pins before you reach them when machining, to avoid breaking the pins or the machine needle.

Needles in a variety of sizes are used for handsewing different-weight fabrics, so keep a good selection to hand.

A cordless electric drill or hand drill is used to drill screw holes through joints, and to make pilot holes for hinges.

An electric iron is used to iron the reverse of fabrics that have been decorated with fabric and silk paints, to fix the paint.

Protective goggles must be worn to cover the eyes when using a staple gun and when using other tools where small fragments are involved.

Right: *1 coping saw; 2 staple gun;*
3 crosshead screws; 4 paintbrushes;
5 crosshead screwdriver; 6 pencil and ruler;
7 tack hammer; 8 protective face mask;
9 rubber gloves; 10 heavy-duty gloves;
11 sewing machine; 12 dressmaker's pins;
13 cordless drill; 14 electric iron; 15 protective
goggles; 16 rubber stamps and roller;
17 pliers; 18 fine copper wire.

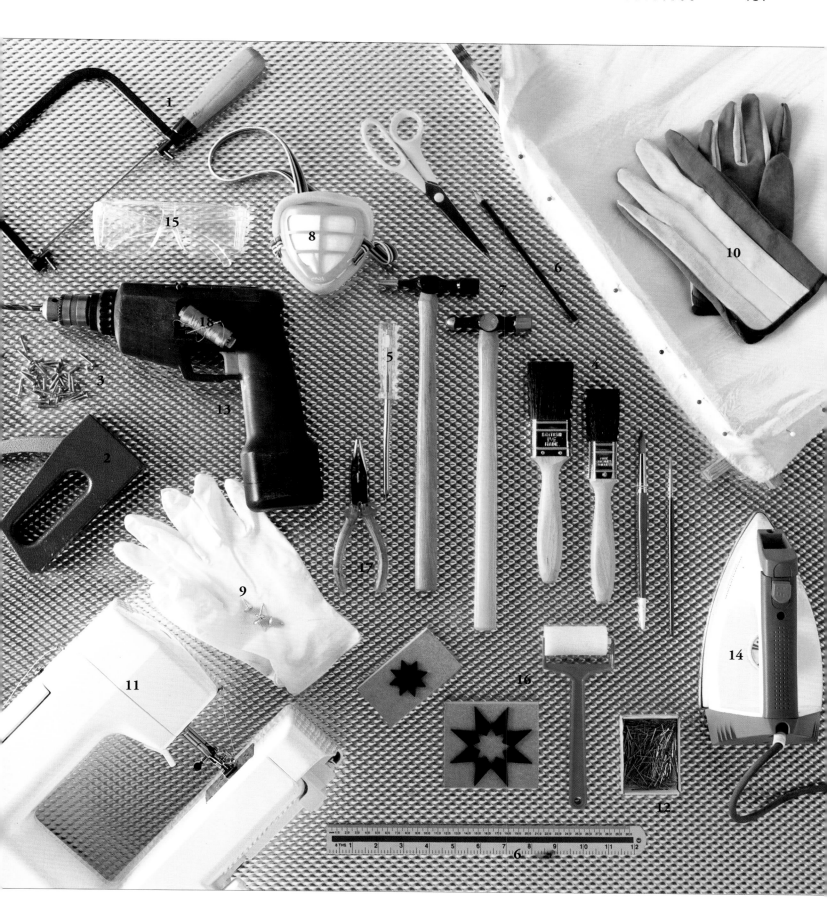

Templates

o enlarge the templates to the correct size, either use a grid system or a photocopier. For the grid system, trace the template and draw a grid of evenly spaced squares over your tracing. To scale up, draw a larger grid on to another piece of paper. Copy the outline on to the second grid by taking each square individually and drawing the relevant part of the outline in the larger square. For tracing templates, you will need tracing paper, a pencil, card or paper, and scissors.

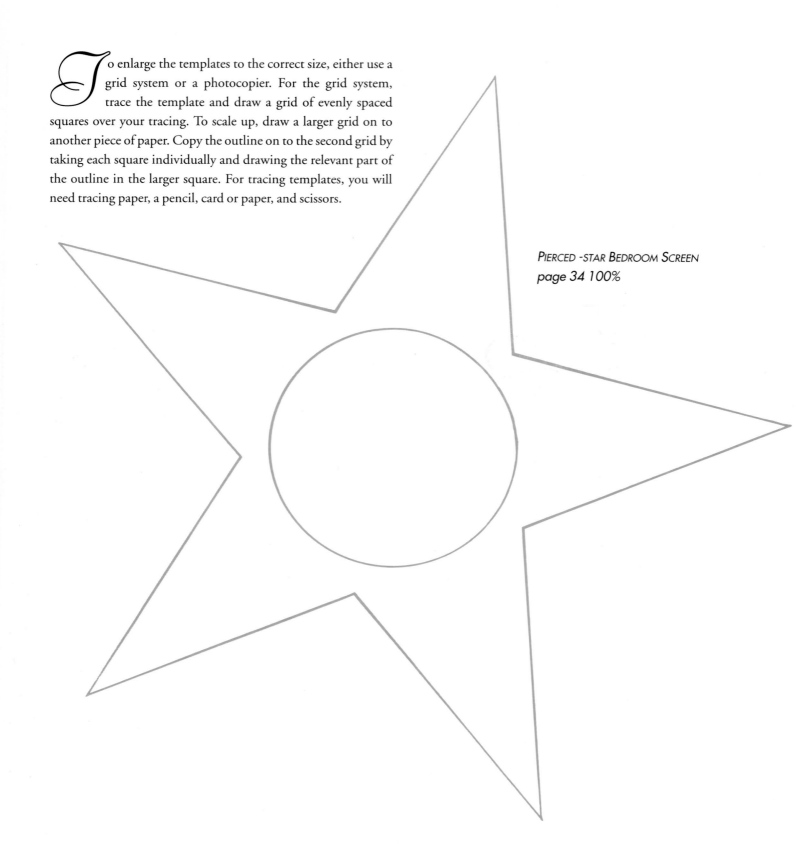

PIERCED -STAR BEDROOM SCREEN
page 34 100%

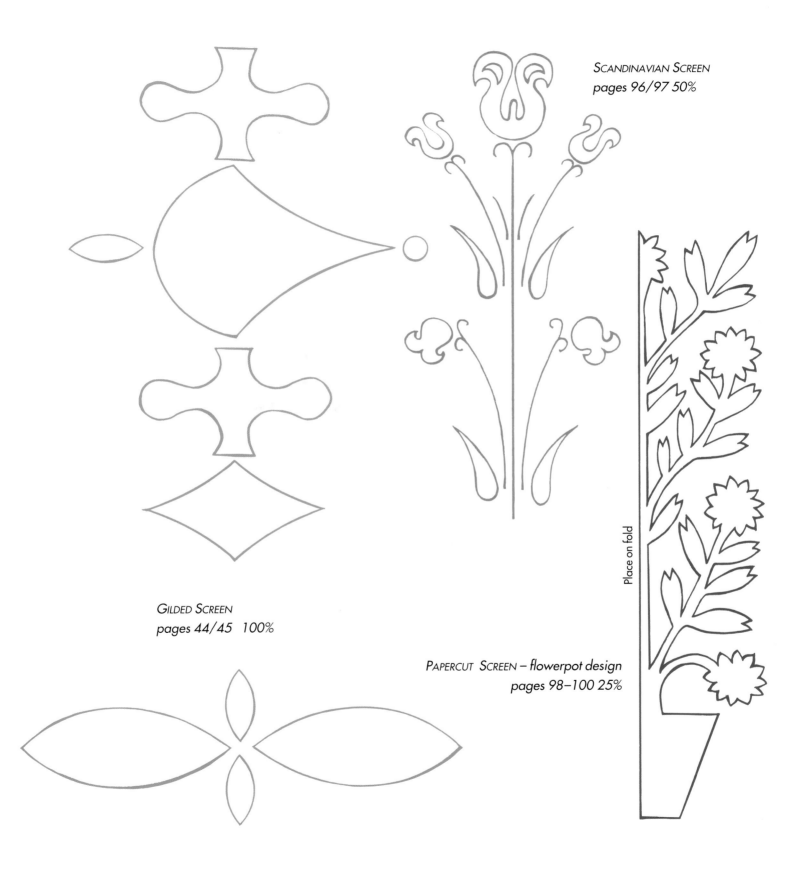

SCANDINAVIAN SCREEN
pages 96/97 50%

GILDED SCREEN
pages 44/45   100%

PAPERCUT SCREEN – flowerpot design
pages 98–100 25%

Place on fold

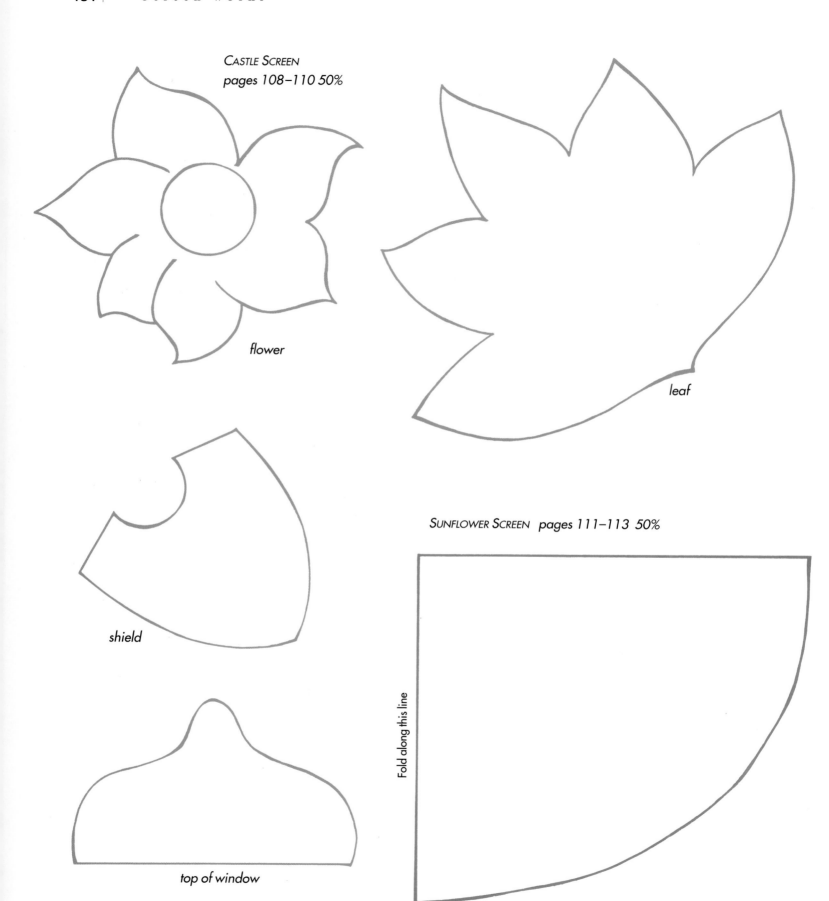

CASTLE SCREEN
pages 108–110 50%

flower

leaf

shield

top of window

SUNFLOWER SCREEN   pages 111–113 50%

Fold along this line

SUNFLOWER SCREEN
pages 111–113 50%

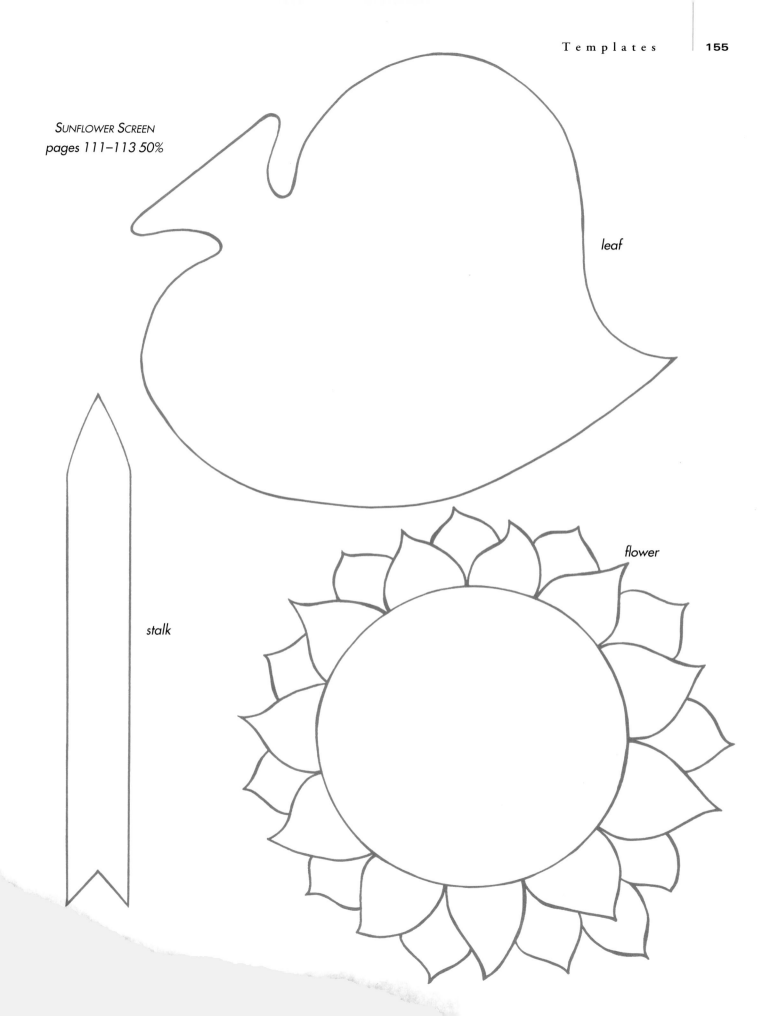

leaf

stalk

flower

ALUMINIUM BUTTERFLY SCREEN pages 122–123 100%

BRIGHT BIRD SCREEN pages 137–139 50%

Fold along this line

Bright Bird Screen pages 137–139 50%

Fold along this line

Fold along this line

Index

Bibliography

The Folding Image, Michael Komanecky and Virginia Fabbri
  Butera (Yale University Art Gallery, 1984)

*Decorative Folding Screens in the West from 1600 to the Present
  Day*, Janet Woodbury Adams (Thames and Hudson, 1982)

The Dictionary of English Furniture, Vol. 3, Percy Macquoid and
  Ralph Edwards (Antique Collectors Club, 1983)

A Short Dictionary of Furniture, John Gloag (Allen and Unwin,
  1969)

The Encyclopedia of Furniture, Joseph Aronson (Batsford, 1989)

World Furniture – An Illustrated History, Helena Hayward
  (Hamlyn, 1965)

All Japan – The Catalogue of Everything Japanese (Quill, 1984)

A Handbook of Styles in English Antique Furniture, Brian Austen
  (W. Foulsham & Co., 1974)

Dummy Boards and Chimney Boards, Clare Graham (Shire
  Publications, 1988)

Suppliers

Ells and Farrier
(Creative Beadcraft Ltd)
20 Beak Street
London W1R 3HA
Tel: 0171-629 9964
(Wide range of beads)

Goodwoods
106 Junction Road
London N19 5LB
Tel: 0171-272 6569)
(Timber and ironmongery)

Wong Singh Jones
253 Portobello Road
London W11 1LR
Tel: 0171-792 2001
(Chinese spirit money and bead curtains)

Moore's Design
The Barn Workshop
Burleigh Lane
Crawley Down
West Sussex RH10 4LF
Tel: 01342 717944
(Dried flowers, preserved leaves, moss etc)

E Ploton Ltd
273 Archway Road
London N6 5AA
Tel: 0181-348 0315
(Metal leaf and gilding equipment)

Scumble Goosie
Toadsmoor Road
Stroud
Gloucestershire GL5 2TB
Tel: 01453-731305
(Ready-to-paint blanks)

Edgar Udny & Co Ltd
314 Balham High Road
London SW17 7AA
Tel: 0181-767 8181
(Mosaic tesserae and equipment)

George Weil and Sons Ltd
18 Hanson Street
London W1P 7DB
Tel: 0171-580 3763
(Fabric painting supplies)

Engravings for Architectural Screen
from Heck's *Pictorial Archive of Art
and Architecture*

Gift wrap for Floral Chimney
Board from Fitzwilliam Museum
Enterprises Ltd

Rubber stamps for the Stamped
Twilight Screen from: *Stampability
- Stars* by Stewart and Sally
Walton, a book plus stamps kit
published by Lorenz Books.
Similar stamps are available from
good craft stores.

Gallery Contributors

Neil Bottle
Tel: 01843-592953

Tessa Brown
13 Charlotte Mews
London W1P 1LN
Tel: 0171-637 2515

Decorative Living
55 New Kings Road
London SW6 4SE
Tel: 0171-736 5623

Sarah Feather Design
Redwalls
Burley Woodhead
Ilkley
West Yorkshire LS29 7AS
Tel: 01943-864500

Susie Freeman
71 Sheffield Terrace
London W8 7NB
Tel: 0171-937 5254

Jason Griffiths
Underwoodsman
Higher Tideford
Cornworthy
Totnes
Devon TQ0 7HL
Tel: 01803-712388

Hospital Metalcrafts Ltd
(Bristol Maid)
Blandford
Dorset DT11 7TE
Tel: 01258-451338

Paul Johnson
30 Queenston Road
Manchester M20 2NX
Tel: 0161-434 1699

The Kasbah
8 Southampton Street
London WC2
Tel: 0171-240 3538

Natasha Kerr
West 11
Cockpit Workshops
Cockpit Yard
Northington Street
London WC1N 2NP

Cleo Mussi
Unit 72c
Abbey Business Centre
Ingate Place
London SW8 3NS
Tel: 0171-498 2727

Nice Irma's
46 Goodge Street
London W1P 1FJ
Tel: 0171-580 6921

Paperchase
213 Tottenham Court Road
London W1P 9AF
Tel: 0171-580 8496

Paint Magic Ltd
5 Elgin Crescent
London W11 2JA
Tel: 0171-792 8012

Amanda Pearce
74 Carlingford Road
Hucknall
Nottinghamshire NG15 7AG

Mandy Pritty
7 Abbot's Place
London NW6 4NP
Tel: 0171-625 4835

Anne Toomey
Tel: 01732-455324

Juliet Helen Walker
c/o 23 Golden Crescent
Everton
Lymington
Hampshire SO41 0LN
Tel: 01590-643665

Lois Walpole
100 Fairfoot Road
London E3 4EH
Tel: 0171-538 5308

Alison White
Ground Floor
Fitzpatrick Building
York Way
London N7 9AS
Tel: 0171-538 5308

Project Contributors
Petra Boase, Sacha Cohen, Dawn Dupree, Sandra Hadfield, Jill Hancock, Zoe Hope, Joan Molloy, Terence Moore, Christopher New, Victoria Richards, Deborah Schneebeli-Morrell, Christine Smith, Isabel Stanley, Jill Tattersall and Allen Irvine, Lois Walpole, Alison White, Emma Whitfield, Josephine Whitfield.

Author's Acknowledgements
I would like to thank Neil Hadfield, in particular, for making so many screens so beautifully and for keeping me on the right track, as ever. I would also like to thank all the contributors for their creativity, enthusiasm and hard work. Additional thanks to Judith and Joanna who made writing the book such a pleasure; John Freeman and his assistant Adrian for all their hard work during step photography; Tim Imrie and Fanny Ward for such stylish finished pictures; John Maddley at Scumble Goosie for providing screen blanks so promptly; and everyone who so kindly agreed to lend their screens to be photographed for the Gallery sections.

Publisher's Acknowledgements
With thanks to the following for providing props for photography: After Noah, 0171-359 4281; Angela Flanders Aromatics, 0171-739 7555; Cameron Shaw, 0171-371 8175; Decorative Living, 0171-736 5623; Prue Bury, 0171-371 5884; Somerset Country, 0171-371 0436.

With thanks also to the following picture libraries: The Bridgeman Art Library: page 11; Christie's Images: pages 8–9, 12 l and 14; E T Archive: page 10 r; The Interior Archive: pages 10 l and 12 r (Schulenburg), and 13 and 15 (Simon Brown).